To Daisy

CONTENTS

AN ADULT WITH AN AUTISM DIAGNOSIS

A Guide for the Newly Diagnosed

Gillan Drew

Jessica Kingsley *Publishers*
London and Philadelphia

First published in 2017
by Jessica Kingsley Publishers
73 Collier Street
London N1 9BE, UK
and
400 Market Street, Suite 400
Philadelphia, PA 19106, USA

www.jkp.com

Library of Congress Cataloging in Publication Data
Title: An adult with an autism diagnosis : a guide for the newly diagnosed /
    Gillan Drew.
Description: London ; Philadelphia : Jessica Kingsley Publishers, 2017.
Identifiers: LCCN 2016043062 (print) | LCCN 2016047828 (ebook) |
ISBN
    9781785922466 (alk. paper) | ISBN 9781784505301 ()
Subjects: LCSH: Autism spectrum disorders--Popular works.
Classification: LCC RC553.A88 D74 2017 (print) | LCC RC553.A88
(ebook) | DDC
    616.85/882--dc23

British Library Cataloguing in Publication Data
A CIP catalogue record for this book is available from the British Library

ISBN 978 1 78592 246 6
eISBN 978 1 78450 530 1

Printed and bound in Great Britain

ACKNOWLEDGEMENTS

I would like to thank Rachel Dormer for supporting me after my diagnosis and introducing me to my wife – you helped me become the man I am today. Thanks also to my support worker Karen Jeans for encouraging me to write this book and never giving up on me. I would never have made it this far in life without my parents, who supported me through thick and thin, before, during and after my diagnosis – I appreciate everything you have done for me. And finally, a massive thank you to my wife and daughter: you are my inspiration and the reason I get out of bed each morning.

Introduction

When I was diagnosed with Asperger's Syndrome, an Autism Spectrum Disorder, at the age of 28, I was sent away without so much as a leaflet to explain what it all meant. As you can imagine, I was left with more questions than answers. What exactly *is* autism? Why do I have it? How can it be treated? What does it mean for my life? How does it affect work? How does it affect relationships? What are the long-term consequences? Can I still get married and have children? Should I get professional support? Where should I live? How do I explain this to people? Why was I not diagnosed as a child? Will things improve?

Unfortunately, there was nobody I could ask and nobody who could answer. As someone whose only knowledge of autism came from the movie *Rain Man*, I discovered to my dismay that there were no books catering for the newly diagnosed adult. The vast majority of the literature on autism focuses on children with the condition, and those books that do cover adults assume you either received the diagnosis as a child and therefore understand an awful lot about it already, or are qualified as a clinical psychologist. I craved a book that could help me understand what it means to be diagnosed with autism as an adult.

Failing to find it, I decided to write it myself to help others come to terms with this life-changing news.

The journey to diagnosis and beyond

The journey to the diagnosis can be a long and arduous one. Before I discovered I had autism, my life was both challenging and chaotic. I bounced from job to job and place to place, trying and failing to make things work. I struggled to make friends or 'fit in', and on the rare occasions when I had relationships with others they were turbulent and unhealthy. My whole life I felt that I was different from other people, but wasn't able to explain why. I was bullied and ostracized, last picked at sports and never invited to parties. I was lonely and depressed, self-harmed and had several breakdowns. I was unable to function in a world in which I didn't seem to belong.

The psychological community misdiagnosed me several times, put me on various different antidepressants and mood stabilizers, and sent me for all manner of psychological therapies and interventions. None of it made sense until one day my mother watched a programme about a boy with Asperger's who seemed in every way identical to how I had been as a child. The more she researched Asperger's Syndrome, the more she realized I fulfilled all the diagnostic criteria. The psychiatrists were reluctant to send me to the Asperger's specialist as they were adamant I did not have it. When they eventually agreed, the specialist told me within minutes that I was 'absolutely on the autism spectrum'.

I therefore know what it's like to live most of your life struggling to fit into society, passed from pillar to post by the mental health community, aware that something is wrong but unable to figure out what it is. I also know what it feels like to receive a diagnosis of autism later in life and the problems you might have adjusting to or accepting that diagnosis. Alongside the relief that you now have a reason for your troubles, it is common to feel a mixture of anger, sadness, fear and shame. I felt very lost and alone, miserable about the present and pessimistic about the prospects for the future, but let me reassure you that being diagnosed with autism does not make you any less of a person and does not prevent you from achieving a place in this world.

The diagnosis is an opportunity to take stock of your life, learn about yourself, and move forward with a new-found awareness of your capabilities. Looking back over my life, I have been able to work out why I did certain things and why certain situations didn't work, and it has helped me explain and come to accept the good and bad things that have come from living with the condition. Some people with autism see it as an illness, a disease, the bane of their lives, and wish they could be without it; others embrace it, and acknowledge that it is a part of them. All I know is that I would not be who I am without it.

High-functioning autism is not a disability but a different way of seeing life, and we should focus on our skills and the things we are capable of rather than the things we cannot do. We are defined by our abilities and our potential, not our problems. Whether you are male or female, young or old, being diagnosed does not have to be something negative – for me, it was the best thing that could ever have happened. Since my diagnosis, my life has improved no end. I am stable, more self-aware, better able to live with my condition. I have a home, I am married to a woman who also has Asperger's Syndrome, and we have a daughter. These are all things I did not think I would ever be able to achieve.

Being diagnosed is not the end of your journey, but a change of direction along the way to a better life ahead. I hope that this book will help you take the first steps towards a happier, healthier and more fulfilling future.

A note on terminology

Since the mid-1990s people all over the world have been diagnosed with Asperger's Syndrome (AS), a form of high-functioning autism that was included in the two main diagnostic tools available to the psychiatric community: the tenth edition of the International Classification of Diseases (ICD-10) and the fourth edition of the Diagnostic and Statistical Manual of Mental Disorders (DSM-IV). However, with the publication of DSM-5 in 2013, Asperger's Syndrome, along with a number of other long-standing autistic disorders, was eliminated and merged into a new diagnosis called Autism Spectrum Disorder (ASD). In order to accommodate such a range of conditions and abilities, ASD is ranked according to severity, from Level 1 (high-functioning individuals requiring support) to Level 3 (low-functioning individuals requiring very substantial support). It is likely that the next edition of the International Classification of Diseases will similarly fold the separate autistic disorders into the single category of Autism Spectrum Disorder.

This change has not been without controversy, and the rate at which it has been implemented depends on where in the world you are living. It is therefore very difficult to talk about the diagnosis in a general sense as some people will be diagnosed with AS and others with ASD. However, Asperger's Syndrome is roughly equivalent to the newer category of Autism Spectrum Disorder Level 1, in that both describe individuals with high-functioning autism and the criteria for each are very similar. This book therefore uses the inclusive term 'autism' to refer to both Asperger's Syndrome and Autism Spectrum Disorder Level 1.

PART I

Autism

THE BASICS

For many people, being diagnosed with autism is a life-changing event. However, it can take a long time to process this new information and accept the diagnosis, particularly when you don't have enough information about autism to know how to react or even what it is you are reacting to. There is often a period of adjustment during which you question everything you thought you knew, which can leave you feeling confused and insecure. It is common to doubt the diagnosis or deny it altogether, and you might be unsure who you should tell, who to go to for help, or even what help you might need.

This part of the book is written to help you during this time. In particular, it explains what autism is, how it affects you, and where to find out more. It dispels some of the unhelpful myths that exist about autism, offers advice for discussing your condition with others, and provides explanatory models that can help illustrate different aspects of autism. It also gives details on the services and therapies that can assist you both during this time and moving into the future.

CHAPTER 1

What Is Autism?

This chapter tells you everything you need to know – everything important, at least – about autism. In particular, it gives you an overview of the condition, explains the jargon that is used within the autism community – that is, people with a diagnosis, their families and friends, carers and healthcare professionals – and helps dispel some of the unhelpful myths that surround this subject.

What is the autism spectrum?

The current thinking about autism is that it is a developmental disorder encompassing a range of symptoms, particularly difficulties with communicating, socializing and understanding emotions. People with autism are placed on a sliding scale of severity known as the *autism spectrum* (see Figure 1.1). Traditionally, at one end of the spectrum is *classic autism*, roughly equivalent to *Autism Spectrum Disorder Level 3*, a condition typified by mental disability and severe learning difficulties. *Asperger's Syndrome* and *ASD Level 1* are towards the other end of the spectrum, and we are often of normal to high intelligence and require far less support in order to function.

Since the term 'autism' historically carries with it the sense of the non-talking, low-functioning end of the spectrum, many people like to stress how close to 'normal' they are by describing themselves as *high-functioning*. Confusingly, in the past *high-functioning autism* was a diagnosis in its own right. When someone says they have 'high-functioning autism', it can therefore mean they are at the upper end of the spectrum and have either Asperger's Syndrome or ASD Level 1, or that they have a specific diagnosis of high-functioning autism. While it is important to be aware of this distinction, you don't need to get hung up on it as high-functioning autism, Asperger's Syndrome and ASD Level 1 are very similar conditions and often spoken of interchangeably.

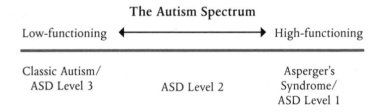

The Autism Spectrum

Low-functioning ◀━━━━━━━━━━▶ High-functioning

Classic Autism/ ASD Level 3	ASD Level 2	Asperger's Syndrome/ ASD Level 1

Figure 1.1 The autism spectrum

What causes autism?

Nobody knows for sure. Some argue that it's genetic and passed on from parents, and certainly most of the people I know with autism think that at least one of their parents has the condition but hasn't been diagnosed. Others claim it comes from influences in the womb, certain conditions of the mother or even some postnatal incidents, but these ideas are still in their infancy. What is categorically certain is that it is not caused by the MMR vaccine, regardless of what certain celebrities and some of your relatives might say.

Is it Asperger Syndrome or Asperger's Syndrome? ASD Level 1 or autism?

Really, it's entirely up to you what you call your condition. There is not yet a consensus on terminology for the ASD diagnosis. Asperger's Syndrome, on the other hand, is variably referred to as Asperger Syndrome, Asperger's Syndrome, Asperger Disorder or just Asperger's, often shortened to simply AS. Sometimes people pronounce it with a soft 'g', sometimes with a hard 'g'. More important is to understand how the autism community talks about it. Many with the condition call themselves 'Aspies', and refer to people without autism as 'neurotypicals' or 'NTs', that is, people with 'normal' or 'typical' neurological functioning. It remains to be seen whether people diagnosed with ASD Level 1 will adopt the term 'Aspie' for themselves or come up with something new. This makes it an exciting, though confusing, time to be autistic.

What is the Triad of Impairments?

People with autism are said to experience difficulties in three key areas, known as the *Triad of Impairments*. These are:

- **social communication** – interpreting spoken and unspoken language
- **social interaction** – the unwritten rules of social relationships
- **social imagination** – understanding how other people think.

While treated as distinct categories, these three areas overlap significantly, and it might be simpler to think of the Triad of Impairments as 'difficulties with socializing'.

How does autism affect social communication?

Most people with autism have difficulties interpreting the *non-verbal language* that makes up much of our social communication – that is, posture, hand gestures, facial expressions, tone of voice. The severity of this problem ranges from those who cannot differentiate a smile from a frown or a hostile tone from a friendly one, to those who have a general understanding of these areas in theory, but in practice get it wrong from time to time. We can also struggle with regulating our own body language and voices, finding it difficult to express ourselves in a way that other people can sufficiently understand. In particular, many people with autism struggle to make eye contact.

These problems are compounded by the fact that people with autism often have a *literal interpretation of language*, and can be rather pedantic about grammar and meanings. For example, a neurotypical person might say, 'Chuck me that hammer,' or, 'Can you run and get me a coffee,' causing an Aspie to literally throw a hammer at them or run to the coffee machine, when what they actually mean is, '*Pass* me that hammer,' and, 'Can you *walk* and get me a coffee.' In order to minimize this confusion, some people with autism use very formal, precise language, leading to a monotonous tone of voice and sentences that don't flow naturally, no matter how grammatically correct they might be.

Another key difficulty in social communication is that, given the literal interpretation of language and problems interpreting non-verbal communication, many people with autism can struggle to tell when someone is being *sarcastic or joking*. When somebody says, 'Oh well done, that was *really* clever,' when they really mean, 'You idiot,' it can confuse a person with autism. Once again, the severity of this problem differs from person to person, and I know numerous people with autism who have a finely developed sense of humour and a hearty appreciation of sarcasm.

How does autism affect social interaction?

People with autism often do not understand the *unwritten social rules* that govern modern life, and may have to consciously process and learn things that people without the disorder learn intuitively while growing up. These are such skills as knowing how to have conversations, forming and maintaining social relationships, and dressing or behaving appropriately for the given situation. Someone with autism may tell the truth – 'Yes, you do look fat' – when by social convention they're expected to tell a white lie; talk when they're supposed to be quiet; or raise inappropriate topics of conversation, such as trying to discuss advanced electrical engineering with the postman, or describing your recent bowel operation at a dinner party.

While most with high-functioning autism desire social relationships, we often don't understand *how to make friends* or how to keep them. Since we might struggle to grasp what is considered 'normal' behaviour, we can sometimes be considered a little 'weird'. For example, while it might be acceptable to swear when having informal conversations in a bar, the same is not true in a job interview. Similarly, we can encounter difficulties when crossing the boundary between friendships and romantic relationships, since the latter are covered by completely different social rules. These difficulties with social interaction can make the social world a demanding and stressful place for those on the autism spectrum.

How does autism affect social imagination?

The third aspect of the Triad of Impairments is social imagination. This is entirely different from conventional imagination, and indeed many on the spectrum are creatively talented. Social imagination is often referred to as *Theory of Mind*, and this is perhaps an easier way of thinking of it. Those on the spectrum are said to find it difficult to imagine what is going on in the minds of others. This inevitably impacts on a person's ability to see things from *another's point of view*, an essential skill in social relationships, and can lead to us being seen as opinionated, stubborn, dogmatic and confrontational. We may also struggle to understand *another's emotional needs*, another key characteristic of forming and maintaining relationships, and can come across as unsupportive and insensitive. Given that we can have difficulties understanding what other people are thinking or feeling and why, many people with autism find it hard to adapt our behaviour relative to the situation or appreciate the effects that our own behaviour causes.

Are there any other characteristics of autism?

Many people on the spectrum have very rigid thought processes, thinking of the world in absolutes of black and white. We can therefore often have a *love of routines*, coupled with *difficulties coping with change*. People with autism will often structure their entire week to a rigid timetable in order to minimize the interference of unexpected occurrences, and can become agitated when this timetable changes. From experience, if I suddenly have to get something fixed on my car, somebody unexpectedly pops round for coffee, or the meeting I was intending to go to gets cancelled, it can throw my entire week into disorder. Of course, while many neurotypical people plan their weeks, it is the difficulty coping with the unexpected and unknown that makes routines significant for many of those with autism.

A large proportion of people with autism also have special interests or *obsessions*, normally involving facts and figures that can be memorized, common ones being animals and the natural world, or vehicles such as planes and trains. For example, as a child I could name every naval capital ship of World War II, the size and range of its armament, tonnage, thickness of armour, top speed, cruising speed, operational range, date of commission, and so on. However, a common feature of people with autism is that while we have *excellent rote memory*, we often have *little genuine understanding*, thus while I could list off reams of facts about naval ships, I could not tell you what they actually *did* during the war or what happened to them. I have met a man with autism who can list the architectural dimensions of every cathedral in Europe, but ask him about the purpose of cathedrals – religion – and he has no idea. The obsession can also focus on parts of larger wholes, such as the windows of buses rather than buses themselves, or lightbulbs rather than lighting fixtures.

Furthermore, many with autism have *sensory issues*, and so bright lights, sudden loud noises, certain tastes, colours, smells and textures can be intolerable to them. I detest the feel and flavours of many different foodstuffs so stick to a very small core of staple foods that I can eat without fuss. I have met many with autism who, like me, can hear like a bat and are highly resistant to pain. Many with autism can be claustrophobic in crowded places, and I am yet to meet someone on the spectrum who likes nightclubs. Furthermore, many of us suffer from *clumsiness*, finding it difficult to play sports or perform fine motor tasks such as tying shoelaces, and we can have a tendency to trip up or walk into things. If there were an award for tripping up kerbs, falling up stairs, banging your head on cupboard doors and walking into doorframes, I am sure that I would win it!

Does autism affect all people the same way?

It is common for people to generalize about autism, thinking one person on the spectrum is the same as all the others and treating all of us as having the same needs, strengths and weaknesses. Indeed, I have met many people who make assumptions about what I am like, my tastes and interests, and what I am capable of, based purely on the fact that I have autism – they normally think I'm great at mathematics or love doing Sudoku puzzles, for example. The truth, however, is that while we share a common condition, we did not cease to be individuals when we were diagnosed. When I first met a group of people on the spectrum, I was shocked by how different we all were. Some of us with autism are confident and outgoing while others are shy and withdrawn, some are friendly and welcoming while others are rude and antisocial, some playful and childlike, others serious and unemotional. How your autism affects you, how you adapt to it and cope with it, is individual to you.

Do all people with autism have special skills?

No! This is perhaps the most pernicious myth about autism – that we all have a miraculous, highly developed ability that compensates for our deficiencies, be it brilliance at mathematics, playing the piano or memorizing telephone books from a single glance. In reality, *savant skills* exist in approximately 1 out of every 200 people with an Autism Spectrum Disorder. These could be mathematical, artistic, musical or memory skills. I have met a couple of people who, upon being given a date anywhere in the last century, are able to say what day of the week it was without even thinking. These are, however, exceptions to the rule. While the vast majority of people with Asperger's Syndrome or ASD Level 1 have intelligence that falls within the average to high range, or even higher, comparatively few of us have savant abilities.

What is the 'hidden disability'?

Asperger's Syndrome is referred to as the *hidden disability* because in public we can seem, outwardly at least, very 'normal'. Many with AS or ASD will mimic the behaviour of our peers in order to fit in. We might consciously learn about body language and how to hold a conversation from books, rather than picking it up naturally. We can play to our strengths, meeting people in one-to-one situations instead of in groups. We can learn to fake empathy in order to meet the needs of an emotionally complex society. The psychological community calls this *masking*, in that we 'mask' our difficulties through careful manipulation of our behaviour and thus hide who we really are. While this might sound slightly sinister, it's more accurate to think of it as an adaptive strategy that many people on the spectrum use to function in a world that is overwhelmingly neurotypical, and a lot of the time we don't even realize that this is in any way different from how other people live their lives.

Is autism a new thing and why is it suddenly so common?

AS was first identified in 1944 by an Austrian named Hans Asperger, and without a doubt the condition predates his involvement, so it isn't in any way 'new'. Most experts agree that the greater number of people with Asperger's and ASD Level 1 these days is the result of better awareness of autism and therefore increased availability of diagnosis, not an increased prevalence of autism among the population as a whole. Whereas in the past, people with high-functioning autism would be labelled 'eccentric' or assigned to one of the pre-existing mental health conditions, today they are placed in the appropriate category.

Unfortunately, it is quite common for those of us at the high-functioning end of the spectrum to encounter people who belittle or disparage our diagnosis as something modern and invented by psychiatrists to keep them in a job, in the same way that they claim that children with ADHD (Attention Deficit Hyperactivity Disorder) simply need a good smack and that 'dyslexia' is a euphemism for 'dumb'. In my experience, the moment AS or ASD comes up, people who are almost total strangers can suddenly launch into quite personal attacks, claiming there's nothing wrong with you and that back in their day they would just suck it up and get on with it so why can't you? Unfortunately, I find trying to explain it further rarely helps the situation, and the best course is to agree to disagree.

Why wasn't I diagnosed sooner?

There are several reasons people aren't being diagnosed until adulthood. The first one is time. Since there was a war on when Asperger carried out his studies, his work didn't reach a wider audience until 1981 when it was mentioned in a study by Lorna Wing, and wasn't translated into English until 1991. Asperger's Syndrome as a diagnosis entered the two main diagnostic tools for psychiatrists – the ICD-10 and DSM-IV – in 1992 and 1994 respectively. Even then, the first people to pick up on it were child psychologists, who started looking for it in young children. If you were already an adult by then, you probably missed the window for the diagnosis. Unfortunately, the wider mental health community tends to be very ill informed when it comes to autism, and since the focus is on diagnosing the condition in children, there is a lack of qualified diagnosticians for adults. This may change as a result of the simplified diagnostic criteria for Autism Spectrum Disorder in DSM-5.

Another key reason people might not be diagnosed until adulthood is the nature of the condition. As already mentioned, we can be very good at masking our problems in one-to-one situations, often using our intellect to overcome our social deficits. Since the meeting with the doctor, psychologist or psychiatrist tends to be a one-to-one encounter in a quiet, controlled environment, we can present ourselves in a very 'normal' manner, making good eye contact and speaking clearly and coherently. Furthermore, many of us with autism can be rather blind to our idiosyncrasies and it takes somebody else to point them out to us before we become aware of them. If we struggle to make friends and therefore aren't close to anyone, nobody is available to flag up our difficulties and so when the clinician asks about our problems we are often unable to express exactly what they are. This is why high-functioning autism is so commonly missed.

Can I self-diagnose with autism?

With the proliferation of health, wellbeing and self-help websites on the Internet, there are growing numbers of people who consult lists of symptoms and take online questionnaires in order to self-diagnose. I have no doubt that, as a result of these sites, there are thousands of people who believe they have ASD or Asperger's Syndrome who have never consulted a clinician or had their problems officially investigated. While I think it is a good thing that more and more people are becoming aware of the condition, and people who have lived their lives undiagnosed are able to seek help as a result of consulting websites, I do not recommend diagnosing yourself. Not all sites are reliable or have up-to-date information, you often cannot verify who made the site, and a complex condition should never be diagnosed through the boxes you tick on a form. When I go onto such sites, they often say I fulfil many of the criteria for social phobia, bipolar, Obsessive Compulsive Disorder (OCD), generalized anxiety disorder, agoraphobia and all manner of personality disorders, which, if true, makes me a walking compendium of psychological problems!

If you are convinced that you are on the autism spectrum as you have many of the behaviours, you may well be right; however, it is not the behaviours themselves that indicate autism but the *causes* of these behaviours. Many other conditions have symptoms that resemble those of autism, and so it takes a qualified clinician to look at the big picture rather than focusing on those individual symptoms. For example, difficulties forming and maintaining relationships might simply stem from shyness and not Asperger's; needing routines could be down to OCD and not ASD; resistance to change could come from a lack of confidence or self-esteem. If you think that you are on the spectrum, you should try to get it properly diagnosed, although admittedly this can sometimes be very difficult.

Where can I find out more?

There are numerous books that provide further information about Asperger's Syndrome, but a far smaller number covering ASD, for which the Internet is a better resource at this time. Probably the most useful and comprehensive book about Asperger's Syndrome I can recommend is Tony Attwood's *The Complete Guide to Asperger's Syndrome* (Jessica Kingsley Publishers, 2015), which covers all the major parts of the condition, including sensory sensitivity. While parts of it inevitably focus on parents and children, there is plenty of coverage of adults, including careers and long-term relationships (though nothing on newly diagnosed adults). Simon Baron-Cohen's *Autism and Asperger Syndrome (The Facts)* (Oxford University Press, 2008) is similarly useful in explaining the relationship between AS and autism, and includes detailed chapters on diagnosis and current research. Both books come highly recommended by the autism community, though if you are after a short, concise read, you can't go far wrong with Attwood's *Why Does Chris Do That?* (National Autistic Society, 2006).

The Internet is a useful though problematic tool for researching autism, since some sites promote inaccurate views while others are too technical for the layperson. Wikipedia (www.wikipedia.com) is good for gaining a quick overview, provided you check the information it contains against other, more reliable sources, such as the Asperger/Autism Network (AANE) (www.aane.org). The websites of the National Autistic Society (www.autism.org.uk) in the UK and the Autism Society (www.autism-society.org) in the US are similarly useful, though these focus primarily on classic autism and are skewed towards parents of children with AS and ASD. The website of Research Autism (www.researchautism.net) provides a wealth of accessible information, and usefully has three difficulty settings – basic, intermediate and advanced – so that you can cater the knowledge to the level that suits you. While its focus is on researching and assessing therapies and interventions, the information it provides about Asperger's Syndrome is very comprehensive, and once you have a more advanced understanding and appreciation of the condition, you might like to return to this site and browse some of the latest theories.

The importance of the Internet lies not only in its access to articles but its interactivity. Wrong Planet (www. wrongplanet.net) is an online community that enables people with AS and ASD to communicate in chat rooms and contribute to online forums. The benefit of this is that people with the condition can answer your questions directly, and the richness of personal experiences can greatly enhance your appreciation of what it is like to have autism and how different we all are. I think interacting directly with others with the condition can also dispel much of the fear and stigma surrounding the diagnosis, and provide accounts that are similar to your own. Communicating with people like yourself can be incredibly useful in accepting your diagnosis, and helps you to realize that autism can be construed as something positive.

SUMMARY

- Asperger's Syndrome and ASD Level 1 are high-functioning forms of autism.

- They cause problems with socializing – communicating, forming relationships and understanding how others think.

- In general, we like routines, don't like change, often have obsessions and can be affected by sensory issues.

- Autism affects all people differently – there is no 'typical' Aspie.

- Autism is not a new thing and people with AS and ASD Level 1 are often able to mask their condition. That's why it's called the 'hidden disability'.

CHAPTER 2

How Do I Tell People about My Diagnosis?

Once you have received a diagnosis of autism, who should you tell and why? This is entirely up to you. Some make a habit of telling practically everybody they meet that they are on the spectrum – from the postman to the person who serves them in the local shop. Others are more selective, while there are some who never tell a soul. Disclosure of your diagnosis – when, how and to whom – can be an extremely sensitive issue, and there is no 'one-size-fits-all' way of doing it. This chapter tells you some of the issues surrounding disclosure and provides short models that can be used to describe your condition in as simple and concise a manner as possible.

What are some of the benefits of disclosure?

After years of struggling to understand why you seem to be different from the people around you, you might be excited to share this news with others. It enables you and the people in your life to explain why things have happened or continue to happen, using the diagnosis as a frame of reference. You can renegotiate how you've been leading your relationships, ironing out misunderstandings that occur as a result of your condition. It can help employers and significant others better accommodate your needs and provide support to make your life easier. And by embracing your diagnosis, being 'out and proud', it can open up opportunities in different areas of your life.

What are some of the disadvantages of disclosure?

Disclosing your diagnosis will change the way people treat you, some only temporarily and some forever. Though things are moving in the right direction, there is still stigma attached to mental illness, and though Asperger's Syndrome and ASD Level 1 are not mental illnesses, they are close enough to one in people's minds for them to think of you differently. Related to this is that autism is very poorly understood in the media and among the general public, and can provoke a knee-jerk reaction. In terms of relationships and career advancement, there can be a very real risk of disclosure affecting your chances, even if this is not enough to qualify as discrimination. There is also a tendency for people to treat you as a diagnosis rather than a person. These are all things to consider before deciding whether or not to disclose your condition.

Who should I tell?

There are a few basic questions you should ask yourself before making any decision about disclosure. The first, and most important, is why you would want a certain person to know. Is it to improve your relationship with that person and deepen the understanding between you? Is it to repair some damage that might have been done in your relationship as a result of your condition, or excuse future difficulties that might arise? Do you want the other party to make accommodations to help you in your everyday life? Or do you simply have a burning desire to tell the person? All are acceptable reasons, but it's always best to know what you want out of the disclosure.

You also need to consider what effect the disclosure might have. Do you think it will improve things between you, or might it have the opposite effect? Some people can be totally fine discovering that you have autism, while others might react with hostility. How well do you know the person, and how well can you judge what their reaction might be? And are you prepared to put in the effort to explain your condition if the other person doesn't understand right away? Bear in mind, it can take weeks or months for you to accept that you are on the spectrum, and it can equally take those close to you a similar amount of time to adjust.

A useful way of thinking about disclosure is to treat it as a series of concentric circles radiating out from a central point that is you (see Figure 2.1). You might decide to first tell the people in the centre of the circle, closest to you – your significant other, perhaps, or your parents. Depending on how that goes, and how it feels, you might then move to the next circle – close friends and family – and so on, going at your own pace and always carefully considering the next step. Remember, you don't need to tell everybody right away, or at all. And you might like to ask yourself if the neighbours really need to know.

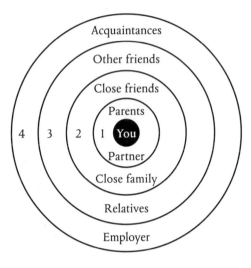

Figure 2.1 Disclosure as a series of circles

When should I tell people?

It depends on who it is that you're telling. The most important thing is not to tell people before you are ready. One of the main reactions I encounter on telling people I have AS is, 'You don't seem very autistic,' or, 'You must hide it well,' or, 'You seem just like everybody else.' Since it comes across that they doubt you really have autism, if you are newly diagnosed it can trigger doubt in your own mind as to whether you really have AS or ASD, or have been misdiagnosed. It took me a good six to eight months to accept the diagnosis, and other people's doubts added to my difficulties during this period. I would therefore recommend not telling acquaintances about the diagnosis until after you have accepted it yourself.

Otherwise, timing is very much a judgement call based on the situation, with one caveat: if you think that your autism will cause a problem or difficulty with someone in the future, it is always best to disclose before a problem arises. Doing so means that you are owning your condition and your actions, you are in control of how your autism is disclosed, and you are being proactive in adapting yourself to the world around you; if you wait until a problem arises and then disclose your autism, it makes it seem as though you are using your condition as an excuse, you won't have control over the timing or manner of disclosure, and it portrays your condition in a negative light.

How do I tell people about my autism?

You will tell different people about your condition in different ways. Sometimes it might be a formal, sit-down revelation; sometimes it will crop up in conversation; and sometimes you'll just mention it in passing. Your romantic partner or close family will obviously want to know about it in more depth than a distant acquaintance, who won't be interested in a lecture on the Triad of Impairments or your love of routines. When you are first diagnosed you don't have the depth of knowledge about autism, or how it affects you individually, so you might think it best to delay disclosure until you have a better grasp of the facts and are able and comfortable to answer any questions put to you. On the other hand, you might feel more suited to telling people up front and then updating them bit by bit as you come to understand it more.

This 'disclosure in stages' is a useful way of thinking about telling people that you are on the spectrum. It is not necessary to tell people everything in one go, at one time.

As a general rule, I tend to keep the first disclosure short. I say, 'I'm on the autism spectrum,' and follow this up with, 'It means I struggle with social situations.' And that is all. Later, if they're interested and ask about it, I might start to explain further, and later still go into greater depth.

It is important to stress the positive ways in which autism affects you as well as the negative ways. There is a tendency to focus on autism as a disability, and therefore to place emphasis on the more negative aspects of the condition, instead of embracing the positives that come from the diagnosis. People at the high-functioning end of the spectrum tend to be reliable, honest and conscientious, often have good attention to detail and excellent memories for facts, are generally task oriented and able to focus for long periods of time on things others might deem 'boring', and will often make connections that neurotypical people miss. No matter how you explain it, however, there are some people who will never 'get' autism. Some people on the spectrum argue that neurotypicals can *never* understand autism as it is something that needs to be experienced to be understood, but I think we should always at least make the effort to explain it.

How can I help people understand my condition?

One way of helping others understand autism in a clear and concise form is to create a short summary that you can give to them. I provide an example as Figure 2.2, which you are perfectly welcome to use. Unfortunately, given that any definition of autism is predicated on how we are different from neurotypicals, the description can come across as rather negative, based on our struggles and difficulties.

Another method that avoids this and is especially useful for employers is to make a list with three columns, one headed 'strengths', another headed 'challenges' (rather than 'weaknesses') and the third headed 'needs', catered specifically for how your autism affects you as an individual. I provide an example list in Figure 2.3.

SUMMARY OF AUTISM

- Autism is a developmental disorder covering a range or 'spectrum' of symptoms and abilities.
- People with autism can struggle to interpret verbal and non-verbal communication, such as body language and tone of voice.
- They often find it hard to understand the unwritten rules of social relationships, so have difficulties making friends or 'fitting in'.
- They might similarly struggle to understand how other people think.
- Autism affects all people differently.
- People with autism can be very good at hiding their difficulties.
- They often enjoy routines and find it hard to cope with change.
- People with autism are not defective – they simply have different ways of thinking.

Figure 2.2 Summary of autism

Strengths	Challenges	Needs
Intelligence	Understanding social rules	Clear guidelines on behaviour
Integrity	Social relationships	Step-by-step instructions
Honesty	Seeing other points of view	Advance warning of change
Reliability	Communication	Reassurance
Eye for detail	Coping with change	Tolerance
Perseverance	Empathy	A mentor/confidant

Figure 2.3 List of strengths, challenges and needs

Are there models I could use to explain my autism?

I think models and analogies are a fantastic way of relating your experience of autism to other people. There are some common ones, or if you're creatively minded you can come up with your own. I have described below three that I have found useful to help me and others understand how my autism affects me.

'An Anthropologist on Mars'

Many people with autism feel they were born in the wrong time or place or even on the wrong planet – some refer to the condition as 'wrong planet syndrome', and several web communities have names that reflect this idea. There are even people that believe autism is literally the result of aliens combining their DNA with that of humans to create human–alien hybrids, but I am yet to read a convincing argument for this! It is a useful gauge of the alienation many feel from society at large, and the depth of their confusion about the social norms that many without the condition take for granted.

A popular analogy that reflects this thinking is 'An Anthropologist on Mars'. The phrase was originally used by Dr Temple Grandin, a remarkable woman with autism, and popularized in the title of an Oliver Sacks book. The idea is that a person on the spectrum is like a human anthropologist who travels to Mars to study an alien culture. The closest real-life example would be a person travelling to a tribal village in a remote land. What language do they speak? What are their codes of behaviour? What is their social structure? What are their ethics? What is the place of the family group in society? What role do rituals play? Which events receive importance and which are everyday?

This is a very good way of illustrating how many people with AS and ASD relate to the rest of society. As anthropologists we are outsiders – observers rather than participants. We study the way people act and try objectively to learn the rules. This helps to explain to people that being in society is not 'natural' to us, and whether we're at work, at a party or waiting for a train, we are always 'on', always trying to figure things out and always aware that we are that bit different from everyone else.

'The Mini and the Tractor'

People at the high-functioning end of the spectrum often have an unusual balance of abilities. Given that most of us with AS or ASD Level 1 have average to high intelligence, people can be bewildered by the areas in which we struggle. A particular problem that many of us have revolves around so-called activities of daily living, those necessary but mundane chores of everyday life. Many people with the condition struggle to remember or even comprehend how to clean their teeth, change their clothes, eat, vacuum and all the other tasks that are essential to survive and function. It is, therefore, difficult to make somebody understand how you can get a degree or write a book but need verbal prompts to open the post and help to fill in forms. The model of 'The Mini and the Tractor' can help to explain this.

Essentially, when we were born, those of us with high-functioning autism were given a Mini while neurotypicals were given tractors. On the roads, we are fine – we speed along and overtake everybody, because they're in tractors and we're in Minis. These roads are those systematic, intellectual, organized things that we do with ease. However, to the sides of the roads are ploughed fields, which are the everyday things like opening the post or doing the washing up. Neurotypical people turn into the fields and continue on at the same speed, because they're in tractors. We turn into the fields, and because we're in Minis we instantly become bogged down. We spin the wheels, and all we do is sink deeper and deeper into the mud, until someone with a tractor comes along and tows us through the field and back onto a road. Then we're off again, speeding along, overtaking people, until the next time we have to venture back into a field, whereupon we get stuck. If there is nobody around with a tractor to pull us out, we continue to spin the wheels until the engine cuts out and we abandon the car. The next day, the Mini is already in the field, so we climb in, spin the wheels and sink ever further. This doesn't mean we are defective – it just means we travel in different vehicles to other people.

'The Filing Cabinet'

When you have autism, you often don't process information in the same way as other people. If you imagine each sensory input, thought or piece of knowledge as a sheet of paper, and the autistic brain as a giant filing cabinet, it goes some way to understanding how most of us operate. Every sheet of paper needs to be analysed, categorized, related to other sheets of paper and then filed in its relevant folder in the relevant drawer before we are done with it. This often gives us excellent rote memory but difficulty combining the pieces of information that are stored in separate drawers. Indeed, we tend to focus on individual details and struggle to see the bigger picture – where neurotypicals see forests, we see thousands of individual trees.

Processing information in this manner takes both time and a huge expenditure of mental energy. Sometimes people with AS or ASD can seem a little slow when you're talking to us, but we're not – we're just busily interpreting all those little nuances of social interaction that neurotypicals do automatically. Sometimes you can say something to an Aspie, and it'll be minutes, hours or even days before they get back to you, because that's how long it can take to work through everything you've said, figure out what it all means and create an appropriate response. And if you give me a list of instructions, I'll focus so intently on the first step to make sure I understand it that I'll switch off from everything you say thereafter.

This is because many with autism can only think about one thing at a time. With a mind like a filing cabinet, every detail is separated and stored in an individual folder. If we're thinking in a certain way about a certain thing – say, the book we're reading – then how on earth can we suddenly start thinking about something else – the gas bill, for example? So we focus on the first file, and the others cease to exist – at least until they come knocking on the door.

And when we try to do too many things at once, or switch from thinking about one thing to thinking about another, we often screw up our whole filing system.

We open a drawer, take out a file, study the page; then we open another drawer, take out another file, look at it; open a third; and before we know it, all the drawers are open, we've got files all over the place, we can't work out what goes where and can't put anything away or let anything go, our thoughts spiral round and round and, unless we manage to stop this process, we can go into what is affectionately called an 'autistic meltdown' – kind of a panic attack and tantrum rolled into one. That's what it can be like having a filing cabinet for a brain.

Should I tell my family about my diagnosis?

Explaining your diagnosis of autism to your family can help ease tensions where these have arisen over the years as a result of your behaviours or misunderstanding of theirs. It has certainly been helpful, in my family, to reinterpret upheavals that have occurred in the past through the framing device of autism in order to gain a new appreciation of why things happened as they did. Going forward, it also allows us to engage in open and honest communication about behaviours and has strengthened our relationships so that we are able to mutually support one another.

That said, it is not always easy either to explain it to family in a way that they understand or indeed to encourage them to engage with the ideas raised. I know people with autism whose parents refuse to face up to the diagnosis, creating problems that need not have arisen. It is difficult to accept that your child is quantifiably different, and there are many who are fearful of the detrimental effect of labels. Siblings especially can react with hostility to the diagnosis, afraid that you will get special attention and monopolize your parents, while there always seems to be the aunt or uncle who does not believe in AS, ASD or the psychological community and thinks it's just an excuse to opt out of life.

Even when your family accepts your diagnosis and is supportive, there is normally a period of adjustment that can cause some negativity. It is a parent's natural instinct to protect their child and when they discover you have a diagnosis of autism, they can overcompensate to the point where it becomes patronizing. Before the diagnosis, I was treated as an adult by my parents; despite having lived 28 years with AS and ten years away from home, as soon I received a diagnosis they started to treat me like a child again, checking to make sure I was wearing a coat when it was cold, that I was going to bed at a reasonable time, that I had eaten enough. They also tried to adapt their behaviour so as not to upset me, but to such an extent that they treated me like a bomb that might explode at any time. If I did become angry or upset, they treated it as a symptom of my autism, rather than something that belonged to me, until I felt as though I could throw a brick through their window and they would excuse it as simply being 'part of his condition'. I had to explain to them that I was still a human being, not a walking diagnosis, in order for them to treat me as an adult once again.

Be aware that there is often a guilt reaction on the part of parents when you disclose your diagnosis. They can blame themselves for having missed the signs, or for making things harder on you. My parents still feel guilty for sending me to boys' camp every summer to help me 'build character' and force me to learn how to socialize, which was my equivalent of hell; however, as I have told them, they did the best they could with the knowledge that they had, and if I did not have Asperger's Syndrome, it might have been the right decision. There is no point crying over spilled milk. Whatever has happened in the past is in the past, and the diagnosis is a chance to move forward and make a better future.

Should I tell romantic partners about my autism?

Most people will share their diagnosis with their significant other. Explaining the diagnosis to your partner carries many of the potential benefits of sharing it with your immediate family. By enabling a closer understanding of the issues facing you, it should make the relationship more successful and encourage open and honest communication that can curtail problems before they arise. It helps to explain why you are the way you are, and if they were your partner during the process of getting diagnosed, you will likely already have discussed with them the possibility of being on the spectrum, so disclosure should not be much of an issue.

On the other hand, as with your family, disclosing your autism to your partner might not improve things, and could in fact make them worse. I would never advocate hiding things from your partner, as intimate relationships, whether neurotypical or Aspie, ought to be built upon a foundation of honesty and trust. However, it must be borne in mind that disclosure could be the last straw in an already troubled relationship, and could be just the excuse the other person is looking for to end things. Similarly, partners can struggle to discuss or accept your diagnosis as it changes how they see both you and the relationship as a whole. Like family members, partners can take a long time to come to terms with what it means for their lives now and in the future, and it can certainly add stress to the relationship. Whether you emerge from disclosure with your relationship strengthened or otherwise is down to a variety of factors and is very difficult to predict, but if you want an honest and open relationship, it is unfortunately a risk that you have to take.

Disclosure of your diagnosis to *potential* romantic partners – how and when – is an even trickier issue and entirely dependent upon circumstance. There are no hard and fast rules in this area, no matter how much you might wish there were. There are many people with autism who are open about their condition and would tell a prospective partner before the start of the relationship, and although this brings with it the risk that the relationship does not develop further, they argue that anybody who is scared away by the fact they have autism is not worth bothering with anyway. There are others who would wait until the relationship was established before raising the subject, but this risks the partner feeling as though you were not honest with them from the start and kept things hidden.

One possible way around this, for both those who are open about their autism and those who are not, is to make a form of disclosure early in the relationship. It does not need to be a formal, sit-down declaration of your condition. You might prefer to slip it into a casual conversation, or make a joke of it. When making a date, you could say, 'Well, thanks to my Asperger's I hate nightclubs, so would you like to go see a movie instead?' or if you make a verbal gaffe, you could shrug your shoulders and say, 'That's my ASD,' and move on. Really, it's down to what you feel comfortable with – if you want to keep it hidden, by all means do so, but be prepared for a potentially awkward conversation somewhere down the line when your partner discovers you didn't disclose earlier. And if you're open and it scares people away, at least you have been true to yourself.

Should I tell my friends?

It might seem entirely natural to tell your existing friends about your diagnosis. After all, they are your friends despite your sometimes odd behavioural traits, and so disclosing that these behaviours stem from autism doesn't seem like much of a stretch. Furthermore, as friends they should support you and accept you as you are.

Unfortunately, it doesn't always work out like this. Prior to my diagnosis I was friends with ex-girlfriends and various people from university who accepted me and my eccentricities. However, when I told some of them about my diagnosis it had the opposite effect to the one I expected. Friends became cross about this modern need to label everything, and insisted my eccentricities were the result of me being me and not some underlying neurological condition that made me 'different' from them. Ex-girlfriends had to examine what it was in themselves that had made them attracted to a person with autism. I lost touch with several people as a result of the disclosure, people I was sure would be in my life forever.

The important thing to note here is that I did not change – the change was in other people's perceptions of me. They no longer knew how to relate to me, or decided I was different from what they'd always thought. This is why it is very important to ask yourself what you hope to gain from any disclosure, how well you know the person and how well you think you can anticipate their reaction. If your autism does not affect the friendship, since you're already friends, you might like to consider whether there is any need to tell them about it and risk changing what already works. Or you might be of the opinion that anybody who cannot handle the knowledge that you have autism is not worthy of your friendship.

This has not been an issue with friends I have made after the diagnosis, perhaps because I have been open and upfront about my Asperger's from the start and so the relationship has been formed in the knowledge that I have autism. Even where friends accept your diagnosis, however, it does not mean that the friendship automatically improves. My wife has several friends who are aware of her diagnosis, yet still become annoyed at her over misunderstandings or what they see as oddities in her behaviour. Disclosure of your diagnosis is therefore not a 'get out of jail free' card or a guarantee that your quirks will be accepted, but just one part of the wider riddle that is friendship, and while it might enhance some friendships, it can have no effect on others or even destroy them. The decision of whether or not to disclose to friends is, like all choices about disclosure, therefore a difficult one.

Should I tell my employers?

In terms of disclosure, this is one of the biggest dilemmas facing adults with autism. Depending on where you live there might be laws against discrimination in the workplace, but unconscious and/or impossible-to-prove discrimination still exists. There is certainly anecdotal evidence that after disclosure to employers, people on the spectrum were passed over for promotion or otherwise sidelined, and that is, of course, always a risk. It is also a risk to disclose in a job interview, knowing that it might affect your selection for the position, but if you don't tell them at interview, and then tell them when you accept the job offer, or on your first day, will they look kindly on that omission? It is a quandary for which there is no simple solution.

If you already have a job, the question you need to ask yourself, as always, is what you hope to gain from any disclosure. If you are performing your job perfectly well, have done so for some time and do not foresee any problems arising as a result of your condition, you might conclude that there is no need to disclose. On the other hand, if you are having problems or anticipate them arising as a result of your autism, do you want your employers to make accommodations for you or give you special dispensations to help you in your job? For example, because of your autism you might prefer written instructions to spoken ones, have sensory issues that mean you need a desk away from the window, or require a mentor that you can go to if you have any social problems with fellow staff. All of these things are reasonable, and not difficult for an employer to provide.

A distinction needs to be made between disclosing to employers and disclosing to co-workers, as these are two very different things. Aspies are often competent, able and skilled employees, but because we can struggle with the social aspects of the job and are deemed 'different', we can often face workplace bullying. If this is a problem that you face, you might wish to disclose to your employers so that they can ensure you are not abused or taken advantage of; equally, you might wish your co-workers to know so that they can understand why you behave the way that you do and prevent any misunderstandings. There are pluses and minuses with each option. If you disclose to your employer but ask them not to inform your co-workers, they can be limited in what they can do to help you, and cannot explain to your colleagues why you might sometimes behave in a manner they consider odd. If you disclose to your work colleagues, they can better understand and accommodate you, but this does not necessarily mean they will treat you any better or more sympathetically. Furthermore, once your diagnosis becomes public knowledge, it will be discussed behind your back and you risk being seen as 'that person with autism' for the rest of your working life. There is also the risk that it gives the bullying type of personality more ammunition with which to attack you.

The Internet is littered with stories about Aspies disclosing their condition at work, and while for some it was a wholly positive experience and improved things no end, for others it is a decision that they bitterly regret. What is certain is that if you do decide to disclose your condition to your employers or work colleagues, and wish for accommodations to be made, then you will need to be prepared to educate them about Asperger's Syndrome or Autism Spectrum Disorder and how it affects you. People with autism need to be proactive and take the lead in educating others about the condition as it is unlikely others will make the effort to understand or empathize with you, and there are some who will never be able to 'get' it. We also need to be prepared to meet people somewhere in the middle – employers can make accommodations for us, but can't change the job into something else entirely in order to make us comfortable. We must make the effort to meet them halfway, and move forward with a realistic appreciation of our capabilities and those things that will always be beyond us.

Who else should I tell about my autism?

This always depends on the circumstances and personal choice. I tend to disclose to people if they need to know, and don't if they don't. For example, if you go to an art class, they probably don't need to know that you have autism, but if you are going sailing and there's a chance you might misinterpret an instruction and run you all onto the rocks, it's probably best to disclose. My wife takes our daughter to parent–toddler groups and has not disclosed to the others that she has autism as it does not affect anything; however, she disclosed to her mathematics teacher as she was struggling to understand, and received extra instruction. So it's really up to you.

The exception to this rule is if you ever have any dealings with the police. It just so happens that the common behaviours of a person with autism – avoiding eye contact, monotonous tone of voice, difficulty recalling specific pieces of information as a result of mental agitation – are the same characteristics the police look for to indicate when somebody is being deceptive. If you are ever stopped by the police, my advice is to tell them that you have Asperger's Syndrome or Autism Spectrum Disorder, and this should ensure that you do not unduly arouse their suspicion. Some organizations give out cards that you can keep in your wallet that say you have autism and what it means, and if you are the kind of person who becomes flummoxed around authority, it would certainly be advisable to get one.

SUMMARY

- You need to think carefully before disclosing your condition.

- You don't need to tell everyone or all at once.

- Think about what you want to get from any disclosure.

- People might not react to the news the way you expect.

- Models, summaries and lists are helpful tools for explaining how your autism affects you individually.

CHAPTER 3

What Help Is Available for Adults with Autism?

Now that you've been diagnosed with autism, what can you do to improve your situation? Many people find it difficult to come to terms with the diagnosis and need help to adjust, while those who are diagnosed as adults often have issues caused by living so much of their lives unsupported. In this chapter I discuss various treatment options and types of assistance that people with Asperger's and ASD can access. These range from psychological therapies and skills training to community support. Some of these treat side-effects of the condition, such as depression and anxiety, while others aim to address our social deficits. Like anything, the treatments all come with advantages and disadvantages.

It is important to point out, however, that by its very nature, autism is not something that can be cured. It is not an illness, and no matter how many times I explained this to my grandmother, she continued to pray that one day God would 'heal' me and I'd wake up without it. The truth is that this is not going to happen. As a developmental disorder, it is part of who I am and if, by some miracle, my autism disappeared, I would cease to have a personality that was identifiable as me. However, we are fully capable of learning and indeed many people with high-functioning autism 'improve' over time until their problems no longer hinder them in society. As an example, I make good eye contact these days, but this is the result of my mother forcing me to make eye contact as a child, my study of non-verbal communication and a conscious decision to make more eye contact. These skills might not come naturally to us, like they do to so many neurotypicals, but they can be learned, and with practice we can achieve what we wish to achieve in life.

This is not to say that a person newly diagnosed with autism necessarily has to embark on this journey. Many people feel we should embrace our autistic identity, and I certainly agree that we should accept who we are. Some people, particularly those who are older at the time of diagnosis and have achieved a happy balance in their lives, might feel they do not wish to change a thing. It is a personal choice, and frankly, if someone is happy as they are then that is fabulous. For myself, I believe that since this world is dominated by neurotypicals, it makes sense if we wish to flourish in this environment to take steps that have a positive effect on our lives. While I am not 'cured', I am in a much better place than I was before I was diagnosed, all through having learned about my condition, accepted it and focused on my strength areas.

Tailor-made approach

Since everyone is different and no two people with autism will be affected in the same way, it is down to the individual to choose which treatments or training they think would be of benefit. I believe, however, that the most useful approach to the treatment of autism is one that addresses both the underlying cause of the problem and the side-effects. What I mean by side-effects are those problems that are not caused by autism itself but are the result of the symptoms of autism. For example, AS and ASD do not cause depression, but the difficulties with forming social relationships that they often do cause, can lead to joblessness, isolation, loneliness and ultimately depression. Indeed, because of their difficulties many of the people I know with autism suffer from depression, anxiety, low self-esteem and a lack of confidence. For some, this can lead to agoraphobia, panic attacks, self-harm and even suicide. Looking at it longer term, people with high-functioning autism, especially if they have lived much of their adult life without a diagnosis, can have problems with self-identity – lacking goals, unsure of their sexuality, confused about their values, and feeling as though they are drifting without any real direction. Many can feel useless, confused, angry and afraid.

If you simply treat these side-effects of autism without addressing the underlying deficits in social communication and social understanding, issues such as depression and anxiety have a high likelihood of returning because nothing has been done to combat the cause. However, if the treatment of your depression is supported by training in social skills that can alleviate some of the problems you might have, the treatment is overall more effective in enabling you to lead a more fulfilling life. Training in communication skills and courses that help people learn how to form relationships will not cure you of autism, but they can help lessen the negative impacts it might have on your life and generally make things easier all round. This combined approach – treating both the side-effects of autism and the deficits caused by autism itself – is therefore worth serious consideration.

General psychotherapy

Psychotherapy is a term that encompasses a huge range of theories, techniques and practices, and these would require an entire book to discuss. From my experience, the most effective types are those that ask us to consciously engage with thought processes since these are such a common cause of problems for those on the spectrum. The best approach for someone with autism, as with anyone, is to identify the core problems and areas that need work and cater the therapy to address these.

One of the best things I was taught through a course of psychotherapy in my teens was to question my thoughts and behaviours. A key example is that thanks to my Asperger's Syndrome I have very black-and-white thinking, with little appreciation of the shades of grey in-between. In friendships and relationships, in tasks I undertook, in my beliefs about myself and the world, I took an all-or-nothing approach. People were either all good or all bad, girlfriends were the love of my life or nothing at all, people were best friends or enemies, and if a task was worth doing, it was worth doing to the exclusion of all else until it was finished. A psychotherapist taught me to visualize a traffic light system in my approach to life, and pointed out that the red light and green have an amber in-between. This has helped me to understand that relationships take time to form, people are ambiguous, and that tasks can be started and stopped and started again without having to be performed in a single sitting. I think many of us with AS or ASD can benefit from a general course of psychotherapy, though it must be appreciated that changes are small and incremental, they take time and effort, and psychotherapy is not a cure-all that solves all your problems in one go.

Cognitive behavioural therapy

The most common form of psychotherapy advocated these days, and a type to which I have been sent several times, is cognitive behavioural therapy (CBT). It attempts to change unhelpful thought processes and thus reduce the amount of depression and anxiety you suffer, and to provide a more measured appreciation of the world around you. Essentially, the idea behind CBT is that situations trigger automatic negative thoughts that lead to negative emotions and behaviours, and so we need to consciously realize when we are having these thoughts and replace them with more realistic and positive thoughts. It teaches you that thoughts are not facts, and that you often jump to conclusions that are not rational, logical or fair.

For example, I was at a castle once and asked a guide if I could go through a certain door. She said, 'Everyone else can, but you can't.' I replied, 'Oh, okay,' and turned to leave, when she said, 'I'm joking! Of course you can go through that door.' I was upset by my misinterpretation, as in hindsight it was obvious that she was joking, and spent the rest of the day dwelling on my mistake. In a CBT session I identified the automatic thought that triggered my upset as, 'I'm such an idiot.' In CBT you look for evidence for and against this thought – the evidence supporting it is that I often make mistakes such as this, while the evidence against is that I'm clearly not an idiot because I have achieved many things. The automatic thought should have been replaced by the alternative (positive) thought, 'Whoops! We all make mistakes and it's caused no harm.' This new thought theoretically would have prevented the upset mood from ruining the day.

Of course, theory is one thing, practice another. Given we often lack self-awareness, people with autism can struggle with the idea of locating abstract automatic thoughts. During CBT, visiting a psychologist in a clinical setting who could help me tease it out, I could in hindsight work out these automatic thoughts; however, in the real world and on the spur of the moment, finding these automatic thoughts and thus correcting a negative mood can be almost impossible. Furthermore, I have to question the basic idea that moods follow thoughts, as oftentimes my thoughts are caused by moods that seem to have no identifiable cause. What is good about CBT is that it instils the idea of questioning whether we are right, and if I feel as though someone is attacking me, I often now ask myself, 'Is he really attacking you, or are you misinterpreting the situation?' Another idea – what would you say to your best friend if he or she was in the situation? – has also been useful. If I am freaking out, I think, 'Just calm down, you're overreacting, don't let it ruin your day.' Given our difficulties and anxieties, however, it is not always easy, and while I think CBT can be helpful for many with AS or ASD, it is not for everyone.

Counselling

Counselling is another commonly advocated therapy, and can be useful in the months following your diagnosis to address the feelings arising from your new situation and knowledge of yourself. Known as the 'talking cure', it usually involves the person talking about their issues, with the counsellor asking questions to shed greater light on these. Importantly, counsellors do not give advice or recommendations – they are simply a sounding board for you to tell your problems to, and through this process come to understand what your problems are, how you feel about them and how you can learn to cope with them. Many of us with autism can feel a build-up of tension and a need to talk about how we feel, called 'offloading' as it is akin to shedding a great weight, and counsellors provide a good opportunity for this. Counselling can therefore be of great use in relieving pent-up tension and offloading anxieties, especially when you have sessions on a weekly basis.

On the other hand, by treating the symptoms instead of the cause, counselling is not necessarily the most effective tool for handling autism as a whole. Many of us can be constrained by repetitive thought processes and a lack of insight into our problems, and expecting us to become aware of these problems and find solutions to them simply by talking is asking a great deal, especially as we often suffer communication difficulties. Indeed, counselling works by people learning about how they think and feel and altering this themselves to find more appropriate solutions, and it can be difficult to think up alternative thought processes or be self-aware enough to understand how changes in our behaviour could result in a different outcome. I have found counselling to be like a plaster, in that it helps briefly when you're talking about it, but does not deal with the underlying wound as it does not address the core problems we have. I would, however, still advocate its use following diagnosis, as this is a time when extra support is often needed.

Mindfulness

Mindfulness is another idea currently in vogue. It is a technique that encourages you to become more aware of your thoughts and feelings, to watch them without letting them control you. It also teaches you to exist in the moment, to become more in tune with your body and the world around you, and accept what is happening, rather than being constantly preoccupied with the past and the future. Incorporating yoga, meditation, t'ai chi and breathing exercises, it is often used in treating people with depression and anxiety problems. It doesn't try to change things, but aims to make you step back from your thoughts and realize they are simply thoughts, not real things in the real world. Furthermore, by becoming more aware of our thoughts and feelings and how they are connected, we can break the cycle of bad thoughts and experiences.

For people with autism, there are pluses and minuses to mindfulness. When things are becoming too much and your thoughts are spiralling out of control, to sit down, close your eyes, control your breathing and simply exist for a few minutes in your own space, focusing on how your body is feeling and the sounds of the room around you, is a very effective tool to calm you down, reduce anxiety and prevent a panic attack. It can also help people who struggle to identify their feelings grow more aware of trigger points, and to understand when they're becoming wound up and when and how to reduce their anxiety when this happens. Furthermore, the idea of accepting things as they are, instead of trying to change or control them, is a very positive idea that can undoubtedly reduce the stress often associated with living on the spectrum.

On the other hand, as it is an Eastern philosophy adapted into a New Age-style Western therapy, I found it very difficult to engage with both the theory and practice of mindfulness in my psychotherapy sessions. The central idea of stepping back from your thoughts and emotions and watching them come and go, without judgement, without trying to control them, as though they are separate from you, was a concept too abstract for me to make sense of. Essentially, which part of me is meant to be watching my thoughts, and does that part of me itself constitute 'thought', and therefore need to be watched also? Which part watches that? Without comprehending the theory, I struggled to put it into practice and don't feel I ever truly 'got' mindfulness. This was not the fault of my therapists but, I believe, a problem with the way my mind works, and so whether it can be of benefit is down to the way that you think.

Anger management

Because of how autism affects us, many with the condition feel stress, frustration and anxiety on a regular basis, and this is compounded by the fact that we often have limited coping strategies and unhelpful ways of dealing with these emotions. Despite the name, anger management courses offer far more than simply learning how to manage anger. They focus on many key areas in which people on the spectrum struggle, such as anxiety, unhelpful thought processes and difficulties interpreting people's actions while offering training in conflict resolution strategies, relaxation techniques and communication skills. I think that many with AS or ASD can therefore benefit from a course in anger management irrespective of whether they suffer from anger, since training in how to cope with stress can make life far easier for both yourself and those around you. What also makes anger management courses particularly advantageous is that there are many that can be done online for free, meaning that those on a budget or who do not wish to see a counsellor or mental health professional can do them in their own homes, though of course you can also attend an organized course.

As with CBT, most anger management courses encourage you to challenge the unrealistic thoughts that provoke negative emotions and lead to negative behaviours. Like CBT, this is often easier in hindsight than at the time, but with practice it is possible to break the cycle of repetitive thought patterns. More importantly, these courses also help you identify the physical symptoms of anger, making it easier to work out when you are becoming angry and act to de-escalate the situation before you reach the point of losing control. They teach you how to solve problems in a systematic manner, and provide conversation examples so that you can better understand how to deal with people in an assertive rather than aggressive manner. They also teach you how to relax in a general sense and how to calm down when you're feeling angry.

It must be pointed out, however, that as with all of the therapies in this chapter, anger management is very much a treatment and not a cure. Because of our autism, many of us will likely always experience frustration and anxiety, and misunderstandings will always be a factor of our lives. However, we can improve the quality of our lives by learning ways of managing our frustrations, dealing with problems without them overwhelming us, and expressing our emotions in healthy and acceptable ways. It is not easy, but if you put in the effort, anger management courses can lead to positive changes in your life.

Medication

While antidepressant medication is named for its ability to tackle depression, the selective serotonin reuptake inhibitor (SSRI) family of antidepressants can help with a variety of difficulties beyond simply depression. These include anxiety, OCD, social phobia and agoraphobia, all of which can be side-effects of living with autism. The basic theory behind antidepressants is that messages are carried from one part of the brain to another using the chemical serotonin, and once the messages have reached their destination, the serotonin is reabsorbed. However, in some people the serotonin is reabsorbed so quickly that the messages fail to reach their destinations. SSRI antidepressants delay the reabsorption of serotonin, allowing more messages to reach their destinations, thereby enabling the brain to function in a healthier manner.

In my view, antidepressants can be of benefit to many people on the autism spectrum. Having been on SSRI antidepressants most of my adult life, I can testify that they dull down your nervous system, making you feel less aware of and less sensitive to external stimuli, such as sudden sounds and physical touch, thus soothing your anxieties and making your thought processes less erratic. Before being on them my mind was like a lightning storm, jumping from topic to topic with bursts of incredible intensity, and I went from crisis to crisis; on them, my mind is much calmer and I can focus on things, see tasks through to the end, and function better in the world at large. The numbing side-effects of antidepressants also help you better control your obsessions and enable you to face your difficulties without your emotions overwhelming you.

There are many myths about antidepressants, and it is important to stress that they are not a cure-all that makes everything better – they don't eliminate anxiety, but keep it within manageable levels so that you're less likely to have a panic attack. Nor do antidepressants make you 'happy' – they simply stop you from feeling quite so bad. Indeed, I find they have a dampening effect that keeps your mood in the middle, evening out the highs and the lows. To be effective, they need to be combined with the various other coping strategies, tools and techniques that can help you take charge of your life, and of course they do not solve your social problems; however, they certainly make it easier to cope, and I feel that without them, I would be far less successful at managing my symptoms.

Antidepressant medication does come with side-effects, and as with all medical interventions, for every benefit there is a deficit. They can make you feel drowsy, and indeed I have been fighting against lethargy for most of my adult life. They also reduce your physical sensitivity and lower your libido, which can have an effect on sexual relationships. However, the use of antidepressants is a trade-off between positive and negative effects. For example, my life before antidepressants was characterized by an exhausting mix of nervous energy, passion, fear and agitation, which was exciting and vibrant but self-destructive and unhealthy; my life on antidepressants is not as thrilling and I feel far less 'alive' than I did before, but it is much more stable and I have reaped the rewards of that stability in the form of more successful relationships.

Any discussion of antidepressants must consider the stigma that still exists against this medication. I have frequently encountered the quite illogical position that it is 'bad' or 'wrong' to take antidepressants, that you should be able to deal with your issues without medical intervention, and that if you do take them you are somehow 'weak'. People can have very strong opinions on this subject, and be very judgemental. My response to this is that I see it as no different from any other medical intervention. Most people, will take painkillers if they have a headache, or antibiotics if they have an infection, and nobody would call a Type-1 Diabetic 'weak' for taking insulin, and insist they should deal with it by themselves. I have autism, a condition that causes me to have erratic thoughts, social phobia and a stressful, chaotic life; antidepressants help me overcome these issues. It is not weakness but a pragmatic evaluation of my condition and a conscious decision to trade the loss of some of my vivacity in exchange for a more successful existence. There is no right or wrong answer here. It is down to each individual with autism to make the choice for themselves whether they think medication might help them or not, and whatever you decide, nobody has the right to judge you.

Social skills training

There are various clubs, charities and private organizations that run workshops and short courses for people with autism to train them in life skills using exercises and role play. Unfortunately, many of these courses are either available only to children and adolescents or cater towards the lower end of the autism spectrum and can therefore feel a little patronizing. If you are diagnosed with autism as an adult, having masked your problems throughout your life, you are most probably already capable of buying a coffee in a café or ordering a takeaway over the phone, so the role plays can be rather simplistic. That said, specific training in body language and how to start, continue and end conversations, and explicit advice on forming and maintaining relationships, is always handy to have, provided you can take from it what is useful to you and disregard what is not.

Probably of more use to the adult with autism are skills courses that do not specifically cater for people on the spectrum. Anybody, autistic or neurotypical, can suffer from communication difficulties and thus problems forming relationships, and there are numerous courses available that focus on improving social skills. They are mostly privately run and are usually targeted at specific skills, such as making friends, interpreting body language, being assertive, improving confidence and learning how to listen. As an adult with autism, I think it is far more helpful to work out where you're strong and where your skills might need improvement, and focus on these key areas.

While your problems with social skills might come from a different place than in neurotypicals, the techniques taught on these courses can be utilized by anybody to make a real difference in your interactions with others.

Study and practice

Depending on how you find independent study, perhaps the most useful way of treating the symptoms of autism, and one of the reasons I was able to go 28 years without being diagnosed, is to research effective communication. There are hundreds of books and websites available that teach communication skills, both for a general readership and specifically for people on the autism spectrum. Learning about body language not only enables you to better interpret others and thus facilitate interpersonal communication, it makes you more approachable because you can send out welcoming signals instead of unconsciously pushing people away. Studying group dynamics helps you understand how groups operate and where you can fit into them. Learning to ask open rather than closed questions leads to more effective conversations. There are guides to help you get better at talking to people, relating to them, listening to them – indeed, if you can think of a communication skill that might need developing, there is likely to be a guide to it somewhere.

In addition to this, many with autism practise to levels that border on obsession, and I include myself among this number. Almost every night I lie awake running through the day's conversations in my head, thinking about what someone said, how I responded, how this affected the conversation, what I could have said instead, how that might have altered the conversation. I practise imaginary conversations in my head, what Person A says, how

Person B could reply, and so forth. Of course, real people almost never reply in the way I have practised in my head, so nothing beats going out into the real world and having conversations, trying to pick up the techniques of more socially successful people and utilizing them in your own speech. How I communicate is mostly the result of a practised repertoire of techniques that I consciously apply when I'm speaking – for example, in the back of my mind I am always regulating the amount of eye contact I make and searching for clues as to when it is my turn to speak. Through this learning and practice, I am better able to manage the symptoms of my autism.

Support

There are many care agencies that provide support workers to help people on the autism spectrum deal with everyday issues, in work, in public and in their own homes. I have had support for many years, since being diagnosed with AS. The idea takes a little getting used to, since it is very hard to admit you might need to employ somebody to keep you on track.

Support is simply that – support. Support workers don't force you do things you don't want to do, or do them for you. Their role is to support you to do those things that you find difficult, in the hope that one day you will be able to cope entirely on your own, though this will not necessarily be the case. In terms of the support I require, my support workers give me verbal prompts. I become wrapped up in my obsessions and either forget, or simply do not bother, to eat, change my clothes, go to bed, wash up, clean the house. While this might be okay for short periods of time, things rapidly spiral out of control. My support workers come in to return my attention to those everyday tasks and keep me focused on them until I complete them. Essentially, I employ them to talk me through putting the washing into the machine, brushing my teeth, going online and paying a bill, making a menu plan – all those things that I realize are important, but neglect. I plan my week with them, including bathing, cooking and shopping, and then they come in for a couple of hours every few days to make sure that I am sleeping, eating, changing, bathing. The mere fact I know they are coming and will make sure I've done my chores prompts me to do them. At my worst, without support workers, I've gone six months without opening the post; with them, I have not missed a bill.

There are various other benefits of having support workers. Alongside their supporting me in my activities of daily living, I talk to them to offload my difficulties and thus clear my mind, which means I don't burden my wife or family with them. Not only are they a release valve for built-up anxiety, they are also a vital lifeline for emergencies – when I wrecked my car by driving into floodwaters, I would not have been able to deal with all the telephone calls to breakdown recovery, garages and insurance companies, or acquire a temporary replacement vehicle, without somebody helping to steer me through the process and keep me from becoming overwhelmed. They are also invaluable for assisting with the bureaucracy that might result from your diagnosis, including meetings and appointments with various professionals who might have a limited understanding of autism, as well as all the paperwork.

Of equal importance, support workers can be used to build up your skills around the community. Whereas skills training focuses on building up skills within a classroom setting, with support workers you can go out in public and practise skills 'in real life'. They can go with you to a bar, the swimming pool, a restaurant, so that you can see how it works, where you have to go, what the procedure is, and build up your confidence so you can do it by yourself next time. For example, I was petrified of going to the public records office for the first time, since I didn't know what it would be like or how it would be arranged, and it was a thirty-minute drive away in a town I was unfamiliar with, so I went with a support worker; after doing it once, I was able to go alone on subsequent visits. They can also help get you set up in a work situation, and mediate for you and support you in difficult or confrontational situations, such as a work dispute, family problem or relationship difficulty.

There are some negatives, of course. Support is only as good as the workers themselves, and while many are professional and experienced, with an understanding of the issues facing those on the spectrum, many are not. Some will tell you about their own lives, which is really not recommended as I don't want to be worrying about their difficulties when they're coming round to help me out with mine, while others have no idea about AS or ASD and so add to your stress instead of relieving it. I also knew a support worker who, instead of prompting people to do things, just went ahead and did them herself, such as shopping for them, planning their meals, doing their washing up; rather than supporting people and empowering them to do tasks for themselves, she was actually making them dependent on her and less able to function independently, which is the opposite of what support is about. Utilizing support workers can also be quite expensive, so you have to maximize what you do in the time that you can afford.

Another difficulty is that while the aim of support is to promote independence, you can inadvertently come to rely on support and use it as a crutch. Sometimes you can put off doing things because you know you're going to be having a support session the following day, so you find that over time you start to do less by yourself than you did before – knowing you can wash up on Wednesday means you don't wash up on Tuesday night, so you amend your routine to fit around your sessions. This is a problem because, along with many other jobs in the healthcare industry, there can be a decided lack of reliability among care agencies, and when a support session that you have at a certain time on a certain day and is part of your routine is cancelled at the last minute, it can cause more anxiety than if you'd never had the session in the first place. Furthermore, if you've then put off your tasks, things build up for yet another day. It is up to you, therefore, whether you feel you need professional support or not.

Financial assistance

In some countries Asperger's Syndrome and ASD Level 1 are classed as disabilities and can entitle you to financial assistance from the government. Unfortunately, accessing financial assistance after your diagnosis is hugely complicated at the moment and is something of a lottery based on where you live, who your social worker is (or indeed whether you're assigned a social worker), and the policies of the local administration. Generally speaking, government agencies find it far easier to cater for physical disabilities or learning disabilities than mental conditions, and frankly have little idea what to do with Asperger's Syndrome or Autism Spectrum Disorder. This is evident in both the forms you fill in and the assessments you undergo, which can often revolve around capabilities instead of realities. It is deemed that if you are capable of doing something then you can and will do it, when that is not the case. For example, while being assessed by social workers I had to undergo an occupational health test to see if I was capable of making lunch. The test was to prepare fried eggs on toast. I told them beforehand that I don't eat toast and that the issue is not whether I can prepare food but whether I *would* if I hadn't planned it, or if I became distracted, or if I'd forgotten to buy food; nonetheless, they came out and watched me make fried eggs on toast in the middle of the afternoon, which I then threw in the bin, so they could tick off their list that I was capable of preparing lunch.

The same is true of assessment forms which ask if you are physically capable of performing various tasks, such as cleaning your teeth or bathing. If you state that you are physically capable of these tasks, you will be deemed fit and well, yet there is little space on these forms to indicate that you require prompts to remind you to do things. Furthermore, there is no allowance for the fact that some days are better than others. All experts agree that there is an 'art' to filling in these forms and that you must indicate on them how you are on your worst day to have any hope of accessing the financial support and the services that you need. Indeed, there are charities that help you fill out these forms and I would strongly recommend that if you are going down this route, you utilize their services.

Not everybody is comfortable accepting public money, and that is an individual choice. Furthermore, there is no quick and easy way to get help as everything takes time and effort, and forms seem to have been written in a way designed to confuse you. That said, I wouldn't be able to afford my support package without receiving money, and given the benefits of support to enable me to live the life that I wish to live, it is an arduous process that unfortunately must be tackled.

SUMMARY

- Autism cannot be 'cured' but you can learn new skills and most people improve over time.

- Many people with the condition are affected by depression and anxiety.

- It is best to identify the areas in which you need assistance and seek out courses or treatment that address these areas.

- You don't have to have any therapy if you neither want nor need it.

- All treatments and support options have pluses and minuses.

PART II

Autism in Everyday Life

Now that you know a bit more about how autism affects people, you might be struggling to apply this knowledge to your own situation or understand the wider ramifications of your diagnosis. This is not an uncommon reaction – one of the difficulties I encountered upon first being diagnosed was applying the theory of the condition to everyday life. Many of the books on Asperger's and ASD refer to symptoms and effects in abstract terms, talking about difficulties communicating, trouble with Theory of Mind, turbulent relationships, problems 'fitting in', but what does this actually *mean*? How does it actually affect you in real life in areas such as work, social and sexual relationships, family and living conditions? What sort of issues does it cause? What situations should you embrace or avoid?

How your autism affects you is unique to you, but there are common issues that most of us experience. The next few chapters describe the potential effects of your autism on various parts of everyday life, and offer advice for dealing with the complications you might face. In this manner, they provide you with examples of autism in action that you can apply to your own life to better understand the impact of your condition and what you can do to make things easier. Learning about yourself and your autism is an important part of coming to accept your diagnosis, and I hope that these chapters will help you to realize that the difficulties you might have been facing have not been your fault and are not insurmountable. With a bit of thought, careful planning, and an awareness of your own capabilities, your autism should not hold you back from being who you want to be.

CHAPTER 4

General Advice and Tips

When living with autism it is useful to have a number of coping strategies. Being diagnosed as an adult means you most likely already have various mechanisms that enable you to function without your difficulties completely controlling your life – otherwise you would have been diagnosed as a child, or at least had the condition picked up on before now. However, it is always useful to learn about other effective techniques and so this chapter details some of the ways in which I deal with both the symptoms and side-effects of living on the spectrum. Of course, we are all individuals, so what works for one person might not suit you. Feel free to accept or reject these techniques based on their appropriateness for your own life, or adapt them however you see fit.

Lists

Most people that I know with autism find lists very useful tools. They fit with our often systematic ways of thinking and acting, minimize the unknown and the unpredictable, and help keep us on track without being distracted by what we consider to be more important. For myself, I have a list of things to do every day, which includes taking my medication, eating meals, brushing my teeth, when to bathe, when to shave, when to go to bed, because left to my own devices I become absorbed in my own interests and end up not eating, not opening the post and not sleeping – I have spent many a sleepless night making a model or doing a jigsaw puzzle. Lists help keep me on track, keep me healthy and keep me functional.

The same is true for lists detailing tasks. If I receive a single step of information on a task, without knowing how it is all going to fit together or the end goal, I struggle to understand what the step is meant to achieve. However, if I'm given a list of all the steps in a process that I can read through beforehand, and know where each step fits into the whole picture, I can do it much more easily. Because of how our minds process information, many people on the spectrum are better at following instructions if they are written down; if somebody tells me the steps to a task, I tend to focus on the first step and immediately forget the rest. Lists also help you to avoid forgetting things, such as when going out to make sure you've turned off the stove and locked the doors, or if you're taking the dog for a walk to ensure you've remembered poo bags, treats and dog whistle as well as the dog. The beauty of lists is that they are free, adaptable to your individual needs and a discreet way of functioning in a chaotic world.

Plan ahead

This is one of the most important tips for people with autism. Given the nature of the condition, most of us feel safe in our routines and don't like sudden, unexpected change or unpredictable situations. From time to time, however, life obviously requires us to fit in other things with which we might not be comfortable, such as attending weddings or birthday parties, travelling to conferences for work, or even going to the dentist. I have found that it takes me a long while to get my head around upcoming events or functions that are not part of my normal daily life, as they always initially fill me with anxiety until I have accepted that they are necessary and I will be able to cope.

My advice is therefore to plan these events as far in advance as possible, and encourage your family and friends to make sure you have plenty of forewarning. With small events, such as going to the doctor or opticians or heading to a bar for drinks, I find a few days' to a week's advance notice gives me enough time to accept the change to my routine and minimize my anxiety. Larger events, such as parties and weddings, require at least a month for me to truly commit to and accept them. Of course, this isn't always possible so I often have to simply grit my teeth and go through with things, but where I can employ this tactic, I have found planning ahead makes things far easier to deal with.

Plan in detail

To me, this is another vitally important part of coping with autism. The unknown can be terrifying for anybody, but for those on the spectrum the anxiety generated by the knowledge that you have to go somewhere you've never been and deal with things you're not certain of can be debilitating. My tactic for coping with this anxiety is to plan in as much detail as I can beforehand, preparing myself for stressful situations by eliminating as many of the unknowns as I can. Thankfully, the Internet is an incredibly useful resource. Maps, satellite photographs, street views and company websites enable you to scout locations in advance so that you know what to expect of the physical environment. Booking movie tickets means you know exactly where you'll be sitting.

I also find it useful to know what time I'm going to get to a place, how long I'm going to be there, when I can leave, what the schedule or agenda is for the day and any other details that can eliminate unknown factors. In fact, planning in detail can enable you to overcome numerous obstacles and function without allowing the anxiety to take over. On a small scale, an example could be going to a restaurant. If I know beforehand what sort of things are on the menu, the prices and whether the bill will be split or paid for individually, I find I am much more confident about attending than if I go in blind. At the larger scale, if I have to go away to a hotel or guest house, I want to know beforehand where I can park, where I can eat, how much it will cost, and the check-in and check-out times – essentially, anything I can find out before I get there is one less thing to worry about.

As an example of what can be achieved with detailed planning, as a shy, anxiety-ridden 22-year-old before being diagnosed with Asperger's Syndrome, I bought a Greyhound bus pass and spent a month travelling across America from New York to Los Angeles. People told me how brave I was, but the truth is that I planned every step of the way to eliminate as many of the stressful unknowns as I could. I knew every bus that I was catching, the time and number, how long it took to reach its destination and the distance, as well as going armed with street maps indicating my routes to each bus station. I booked every hostel and motel I was staying in, planned which locations in each city I would visit on which days, how much they cost and the walking distance between each. I ate in fast food restaurants with which I was familiar, since the anxiety about whether a restaurant was table service or self-serve was too great for me. Admittedly, I returned after the month having had only a handful of conversations, since I was terrified of talking to other people, but I had achieved my goal of crossing by land from the Atlantic to the Pacific Oceans. Detailed planning can therefore enable you to do things that you never believed you could be capable of.

Alternative plans

Thanks to our often rigid thought processes, many people with autism struggle to deal with the unexpected, and so making alternative plans or even having an arsenal of pre-prepared strategies to cope when things go wrong can be very useful. For example, if I plan to eat a bacon sandwich for lunch, but upon going to the store where I normally buy my bacon they have sold out, I lack the flexibility to buy the bacon elsewhere and am unable to think up an alternative on the spot, so end up missing lunch. This example is a common one among people on the spectrum, and having an alternative plan – such as, if they don't have bacon I will buy chicken slices – helps to avoid going hungry. Another solution is to keep a tin of tuna and packet of rice in the cupboard, so that if ever my lunch plans fall through, I can apply the backup plan of tuna and rice.

It might be time-consuming, but the same alternative preparations, combined with detailed planning, can greatly reduce anxiety in unknown or stressful situations. In the example of planning what you'll eat at a restaurant beforehand, you can select a second option in case when you arrive they have run out of your main choice. When catching a bus it is useful to research the times of the subsequent bus in case yours is either cancelled or full; that way, you know already whether you have time to do what you wanted to do and don't need to alter your plans on the fly. Alternative plans can eliminate being thrown into an unknown situation and the often negative decisions we make while in that anxious state, and so it is certainly something worth considering by anybody with autism.

Satellite navigation/GPS

In a similar fashion, I find satellite navigation/GPS to be a must in my car. Like many people on the spectrum, I take set routes to and from a place. I may know of other routes, having been driven by other people, and be able to work out routes by myself, but I will rigidly stick to my own regular route. If I come to a place where the road is closed as a result of an accident, I struggle in that moment to change my intended route and find my way to my destination. Before I got GPS, I would often simply turn around and go home, which is not ideal if the trip is important. By providing alternatives at the press of a button, GPS has enabled me to reach my destination in a relatively calm manner when I have been faced with a blockage, both physical and mental.

Fast getaway

This is a strategy I employ to help avoid being overwhelmed by anxiety at social events. From my teens I avoided alcohol and learned to drive so that I would always be able to leave a social situation if it became too much for me and have the means to get home quickly and safely. Indeed, I find that just the knowledge that I can leave, should I want to, makes social situations far less stressful, avoiding the panic reaction of feeling trapped and out of control. This is helped by ensuring the car is parked in an accessible place, not blocked in by other party-goers, or keeping enough money in reserve for the train fare or taxi should I need it. Furthermore, I find sitting towards the end of a table instead of the middle means you can get up and slip away without it being noticed by the group at large. This is made much easier if you have a confidant seated beside you who knows that you have autism, to whom you can give your share of the bill before you leave and who can make excuses for you. The ability to escape from a social situation is therefore a very useful tactic for people with autism to employ.

Time out

Time outs are equally useful for dealing with the pressures of social situations. While sometimes you might need to get right away, using the fast getaway technique, sometimes it is enough to calm your anxieties to take a 'breather' for a few minutes by strolling around the block or heading out into the garden to sit by yourself. It can help to have a 'safe place' where you can retreat for a time to relax and calm down before returning to the social situation. When I was young I lived opposite the back gate of school so returned to my house at lunchtime to de-stress and prepare myself to face the afternoon. At work, I would find a bench where I could retreat from my co-workers, or else I would sit in my car, close my eyes and take some deep breaths. While some might find this behaviour odd, I think those of us with autism should not be criticized for doing whatever enables us to fit into a neurotypical world. It takes a lot of energy to act 'normal' around other people, and these time outs are often necessary to avoid us becoming overwhelmed.

Deferred decisions

In order to avoid feeling obligated to attend uncomfortable social situations or consenting to attend events that are so near I don't have time to get my head around them, provoking much anxiety, I never make a decision upon a future engagement at the initial point of asking. The pressure of being expected to make a decision on the spot that I might later regret is something that fills me with dread, and because I'm instantly on the defensive, I'm anxious and unsure, and I can never think clearly at the time. Therefore, upon being invited to something, my first response is invariably, 'I'll think about it.' This is true, because I will go away and think about it when I have calmed down, and make an informed decision whether or not it is something I feel comfortable doing. While the person doing the inviting might try to coerce you to make the decision right away, there is nothing wrong with taking the time to make the decision that suits you. Another, equally useful response is, 'I'll check my calendar.'

Just say 'no'

I also find that at times I'm just not up to the pressures of attending social events or mixing with people. In these situations, there is nothing wrong with being honest and simply admitting that you do not wish to go. Well into my twenties I agonized over making up excuses to avoid going to bars or clubs, faking car trouble, complaining of illness, saying I had a prior engagement, and all manner of 'acceptable' reasons not to attend. Then I realized that nobody has the right to make you do something you don't want to do. It sometimes does not go down well if you say you don't want to go to something, but it is the truth and you don't have to offer reasons. If a person is a true friend, you don't need to make excuses – 'I don't want to' is perfectly acceptable. I have friends who like to go out for a meal followed by a nightclub, and in this situation I will join them for the meal but go home when they head off to the club, as I know that is something I don't enjoy. We are all different, and as someone with autism who has thought about this a great deal, I know what situations I'm comfortable with and those that I'm not.

Stock phrases

At its simplest, this is preparing responses to potential questions, such as, 'If they ask me how the kids are, I'll say they're excited about starting school.' At its more complex, it is learning a number of phrases you can employ in different situations to help ease your social difficulties and mask your condition, should you wish to do so. I find both techniques, to a certain extent, help me overcome the anxieties of social situations. You can come up with your own or find them in books on effective communication, but I'll provide a few examples here.

Starting conversations with acquaintances or strangers is difficult without knowing the unwritten rules of these interactions, and preparing stock phrases can help here. When meeting people, the first question is often, 'Hi, how are you?', which takes pressure off having to think something up; but if they ask it first or reply, 'Fine, thanks, how are you?', I know a lot of people with autism who either take this question literally or are too honest and will describe exactly how they are, when the person isn't actually interested in how they are – the question is simply a tool to start a conversation. While I'm not really comfortable replying with the ubiquitous 'Fine, thanks', when I'm anything but fine, the phrases 'I can't complain', 'I'm hanging in there' and 'Still breathing' are ambiguous enough to be truthful, regardless of how you actually are, yet provide a socially appropriate answer. Another technique is to deflect the question back onto the person and let them talk, as in, 'Not bad, thanks, how are you?'

In these initial stages, a follow-up question is normally, 'So, what have you been up to?' I know somebody with autism who always panics when people ask him that as his mind goes blank and he tries to recall what he's been doing, what was important and what wasn't, what he should mention and what's appropriate, and he stands in silence. Others struggle to avoid the literal interpretation of the question and start reeling off the fact that they got up, had a coffee, had some breakfast, had a shower, which the other person doesn't want to know. To take the pressure off, my response to this question is normally, 'Oh, you know, a bit of this, a bit of that, how about you?' to deflect the question back onto them. Otherwise, I prepare a response before going into a social situation by working out the salient points of my recent experience, such as holidays, special events or achievements, and mention those.

Early in any conversation with a stranger, you can often ask, 'So, what do you do?' and from their answer expand onto different topics. Unfortunately, I find that it can be rather awkward and confusing to be on the receiving end of this question. The answer is that I worked many years without a diagnosis and as a result had a breakdown and lost my job before being diagnosed with Asperger's Syndrome, and have since then been trying to rebuild my life and confidence and am terrified of going back into a work situation and having another breakdown, so have done some university study and hope to make a living from writing. Of course, that is far too long and convoluted an answer for somebody who was simply making initial small talk and was expecting the response, 'I'm a fireman,' or, 'I work in local government.' To avoid the awkwardness, I tend to say, 'I'm taking some time off to work on myself,' 'I'm a student,' or, 'I'm a struggling writer,' all of which are true and to the point. I used to say, 'I'm currently between things,' but that was sometimes followed by the question,

'Between what and what?', which forced me into the deeper explanation of my breakdown and diagnosis with autism, which tends to be something to avoid when first meeting people.

Stock phrases can be used deeper in conversations. Since I don't always follow what people are saying, I regularly ask them to clarify what they mean in a manner that I hope makes me sound interested and not simply confused. As a teen I would always say, 'In the sense of...?' and trail off to encourage them to expand on the topic. However, people started to notice that I said this multiple times a conversation, so I supplemented it with, 'How do you mean?' and 'In what way?' In this way, you are asking them to say what they've just said in a different way, or go into detail to explain something you've not understood, while covering up the fact that you've got no idea what they're talking about. If I still don't understand, I tend to fixate on one thing they have said that I did understand and steer the conversation back towards that, but then I'm sure we all have techniques to keep things moving.

Another tactic I use, more often with strangers than friends, is employing words or phrases with ambiguous meanings. I regularly use the word 'indeed' when I'm not sure what response I'm supposed to give. If somebody makes a comment and I can't work out if it's meant to be taken seriously or as a joke, or if I'm meant to reply with a 'yes' or a 'no', I simply cock my head to one side and say, 'Indeed.' The speaker can then read into my response whatever they wish. For example, if someone says, 'Beautiful day, isn't it?' and to me the day seems no different from any other, I say, 'Indeed,' since it could mean I agree that the day is beautiful, or it could mean that I'm playing along with the joke that the day isn't beautiful at all. The word 'absolutely' works well here too.

There are numerous different ways in which you can answer questions or cope with uncomfortable situations thrown up by the communication difficulties that might result from your autism. Learning stock phrases therefore has the benefit of reducing anxiety, easing conversation, masking your social difficulties (if you wish to do this) and generally making communication more effective. I'm not advocating you speak like a robot and use only a handful of repetitive phrases when communicating, simply that it is helpful to have tools to get through those moments when you get stuck.

Multiple purchases

Many people on the spectrum have favourite articles of clothing to which they can become rather attached. In the past I have had favourite shirts or shorts which I wear as long as I can, put in the wash, dry and put straight back on. The trouble is, after a year or so I will have worn out the clothes and then when I go back to the shop for another, I discover they no longer stock that product and have to select something new, which is never as comfortable as the clothing I had. Indeed, I can remember T-shirts I used to own that I miss after 20 years. To get around this obstacle, if I find a piece of clothing or a pair of shoes I particularly like, I buy three of them, wear one and keep the other two in the wardrobe until I have wrecked the original set. Of course, this only delays the inevitable since after having worn out every set, you still have to move on to new clothing, but it means you don't need to switch to new clothes so frequently. Obviously, this is something that won't suit everybody – if you keep up with rapidly changing fashions or are into expensive clothing, buying three of everything is more hindrance than help, but I think this tip can certainly help some people.

Goal-oriented association

If you want to have social contact and possibly form relationships of both the platonic and romantic varieties, but struggle to deal with purely social situations, I have found that goal-oriented group activities can help us overcome our social weaknesses. I have always struggled in situations where there is no goal other than to socialize, such as going to a bar or nightclub or dinner party, where there are no rules about how the interaction is going to be managed and the relationships between people are not defined. However, when the group is engaged in an activity in which we are working towards a specific aim and have allocated roles, it takes the pressure off having to socialize for the sake of socializing, enabling you to relax and ease yourself into it.

For example, when I was younger I volunteered as a crewmember on a tall ship that sailed across the Atlantic for 25 days. Divided into three watches for the duration of the voyage, you worked, ate and slept with your watch mates. In this situation, we had a joint goal (sailing the ship), we had been assigned to the watch so were bound together by work ties rather than social ones, and as we rotated roles from helm to lookout or worked together on the masts or raised and trimmed the sails, we knew how we fitted together and it was easy to feel a part of the whole without being overwhelmed by the need to simply socialize. However, as soon as we reached the Caribbean, the crew divided into friendship groups to explore the islands, and without the structure and assigned roles, I was unable to understand where I fitted in, who to hang around with, what to do or what to talk about. Without a common goal to unite us, I lost my place in the group.

Similar, more everyday examples might be joining an amateur dramatics group, volunteering in a charity shop or taking an evening class. Since you have a goal to work towards and a role in the theatre production, shop or class, you can focus on the task alongside the rest of the group without the expectation of being sociable. However, it is inevitable that you will have conversations with the people around you as a secondary effect of doing the task, which means you gradually build relationships through shared activities without the pressure of setting out to make friends. When people invite me to picnics or barbecues, I am filled with anxiety because there is no structure to the interaction; if they invite me bowling, on the other hand, I feel much easier about the occasion as I know what is expected of me and it takes the focus off socializing and onto doing a task. Therefore, I would wholeheartedly recommend people with autism seek out goal-oriented interactions if you want social contact but find socializing uncomfortable.

Don't let fear control your life

It is very easy to allow fear of situations or outcomes to restrict your opportunities. After the diagnosis of autism, people such as family can want to wrap you in cotton wool so that you never again experience negative stimuli. What they fail to realize is that by cutting you off from the risks of bad experiences, and always looking at the worst-case scenario, they prevent you from experiencing the good. I was always afraid of having a baby, worrying that I wouldn't be able to cope or that it would have autism or experience depression. By trying to avoid these negative possibilities, I had overlooked the possibilities that I might be able to cope, it probably wouldn't have autism or experience depression, and even if it did, it wouldn't be the end of the world. I could easily have allowed fear of being on the spectrum ruin one of the best things I have ever done.

GENERAL ADVICE AND TIPS

This is not to say that I lost my fear. Indeed, courage is not the absence of fear but the ability to feel the fear without letting it stop you from doing what you want. If there is something that you want to do, don't allow fear of not being able to do it because of your autism prevent you from trying. Sometimes things are beyond us, so I am not talking about going to a nightclub if you hate the noise, hustle and bustle of a crowded nightclub. However, if you want to go to the movies, but have nobody to go with, go by yourself, no matter how awkward or uncomfortable it feels. I spent years afraid to go to the movies until I forced myself to do this. I would arrive late to avoid having to stand around by myself, book a seat by the aisle, watch the movie and leave quickly. I always felt anxious, but I was able to watch movies that I wanted to see. Feel the fear, but do it anyway.

Make yourself comfortable

My final tip is to do what makes you feel comfortable, whatever that may be. I believe that if something makes it easier to live your life with autism in a neurotypical world, then provided it doesn't harm anybody else, go ahead and do it. If wearing sunglasses indoors makes you feel more confident because you don't have to worry about eye contact, do it. If wearing earplugs enables you to be around a screaming baby, put them in. If you don't like communicating on the phone as you get flustered, and prefer to use text messages or e-mail, then use text messages or e-mail. I have done and regularly do all three of these examples, and I admit you might get strange looks, people might think you're eccentric, but if it enables you to go to that place, be around that baby, communicate in a coherent manner, then who has the right to tell you to take off your sunglasses, or remove your earplugs, or speak to them on the phone? Do what you need to do to function, to manage, to be all you can be, and if somebody else has a problem with it, it doesn't matter, because the person who best understands what helps you cope is you.

SUMMARY

- Lists are very effective tools for coping with autism.
- Plan, plan, plan, and make alternative plans as well.
- Don't be afraid to say 'no', take a time out or simply leave a social situation if you need to.
- Having a common goal or task is a good way to ease the pressures of socializing.
- Preparing stock phrases can take the fear out of conversations.
- If you can afford it, multiple purchases can postpone the stress of replacing favourite items of clothing.
- Feel the fear, but do it anyway.
- Do what makes you feel comfortable.

CHAPTER 5

At Home with Autism

Having lived in various situations – alone, with parents, friends, strangers and partners, and in an assisted living house – both before and after my diagnosis, I have experienced the range of benefits and disadvantages of living in different ways with autism. While they all have positives and negatives, some are better for those living with the condition and some I would recommend against. As always, however, we are all individuals and what might suit one person might not fit with another. While many on the spectrum will spend their whole lives at home with their parents, others will move a number of times into different situations. Since you do not always have a choice about where or how you live, knowing the possible benefits and drawbacks of certain living situations can help you plan for the future or accept what you cannot change, and it is with this in mind that I have written this chapter.

General requirements

Most people with autism like the home to be a safe place where we can retreat from the social neurotypical world and recharge our batteries. For those with an attachment to objects as much as or sometimes more than other people, home is the place we keep those things that comfort us – our books, our stamp collections, our computers, or whatever else soothes us. It is the place where we often carry out our obsessions and practise our rituals, and so needs to be free from distractions and intrusions. Furthermore, given our possible sensory issues, a place with the right textures, colours, and levels of noise and light is important.

While different people have different needs, most people with autism require a place, whether a room or the whole home, to which we have exclusive access. This eliminates the stress of having to share our things with others or indeed the fear of other people touching our belongings when we are not around. For example, I hate sharing kitchens with other people, and found that when living communally I would keep a knife, fork, teaspoon and dessert spoon in my food cupboard rather than the cutlery drawer so that I would be the only one using them and they would always be there when I needed them. Furthermore, I had a lock on my door that would always be fastened if I left.

It is also useful to have a place where we don't have to worry about people knocking on the door or ringing us up and interrupting us. In one shared house I lived in, I put a sign on the door requesting people not to knock – if the door was closed, it meant that I didn't want to be disturbed, while if it was ajar, they were welcome to enter. This is because I needed a safe place where I could shut myself off and lose myself in a movie or a book or some music without the fear of social contact; otherwise, I couldn't relax and worried constantly about somebody knocking on my door and demanding my attention when I didn't feel ready or able to give it.

In terms of decor and sensory issues, these are down to the individual. Many people on the spectrum cannot abide certain colours or textures or combinations of the two. I have very sensitive hearing and find it difficult to cope with noise that intrudes into my home. If there is a busy road, a noisy party, or upstairs neighbours with heavy feet, I can become very agitated, whether it is day or night. Indeed, in one house where I could hear a neighbour's television followed by his snoring every night I barely slept for five months as I couldn't distract myself from the sounds I was hearing, even with earplugs. If the sound violates our safe haven, preventing us from relaxing, this can have a knock-on effect on our tiredness and our mood and ability to function. It can also make us feel very vulnerable, as though open to attack. By the end of that five-month period I was a nervous wreck.

When living in flats, there are a number of factors that can help someone with autism to cope. Having lived in many places, I have found that an allocated parking space is a must-have as I was nervous every time I returned home in case there was nowhere to park. The downside to this is that if somebody parked in my parking space, I became incredibly disturbed, unable to settle or rest until they had moved, which, if it was over a weekend, meant a very stressful few days. I was more settled in those blocks that employed a concierge who could help resolve problems, and just the knowledge that he was there should I need him was a great source of comfort. In a similar way, if you have a good landlord then it reduces anxiety, though as with anything, some landlords are better than others. Spyholes, entry-phone doors and CCTV can help us feel more secure and regulate the people who wish to intrude upon our time.

Living with family

According to various studies, around half of the adults at the high-functioning end of the autism spectrum live at home with their parents. I am not sure whether this applies to people diagnosed as adults or whether these surveys are swayed towards the much larger proportion of people diagnosed as children who do not move out of the family home when they reach adulthood. Whatever the case, I do know many people with autism of varying ages who live with their parents. Not everyone has supportive parents and sometimes the difficulties of the parent–child relationship, differing expectations and personality clashes make it impossible to live at home. In today's economic climate, however, people living at home into later life or indeed moving out and returning home several times is much more common than it once was and has lost much of the stigma it used to have.

There are many advantages to living at home, and for a person on the autism spectrum this can seem like the perfect living situation. By the time you are an adult the family is used to your idiosyncrasies and often caters for them or manoeuvres around them, and so it can provide a relatively sheltered, stable life without excessive surprises or added stresses. With family on location there is plenty of support on hand in every aspect of your life, from self-care and activities of daily living to social and career advice. It avoids the uncertainties of living with strangers or alone. It is also a good, stable base from which to launch into more independent living, if that is your choice, and a safety net into which you can return if things do not work out as intended.

However, while there is nothing wrong with living at home with family, it is easy to become dependent upon home comforts, which can be counterproductive in the long term. I have heard people with autism say that they'll live with their parents all their lives and will commit suicide when their parents die, which is obviously not an ideal situation in which to find yourself. When returning home to live with my parents after my diagnosis, I struggled to improve my self-care skills because my parents, through no fault of their own, were very keen to be parents, my mother taking over with the cooking and cleaning, while my dad sorted out my car for me and dealt with my finances. Since I had enough social contact from them, I did not have to try and make friends or engage with the wider world. Living with family can therefore make you less able to function independently, and I would certainly recommend all parties in this arrangement be made aware of this and take steps to ensure that a certain level of independence can be attained. Even then, it is very difficult to practise living independently when you are in a family household.

A few months after my diagnosis I was offered a choice between remaining at home with my parents and taking a room in an assisted living house. On the one hand, I felt that I would be perfectly happy staying at home as I was, studying one course after another through distance learning and living a safe, happy, sheltered life; on the other, I knew that moving out would enable me to learn independent coping skills, open up more opportunities and enable me to become a part of wider society. It is certainly not an easy decision to make, and nobody can make it for you. Moving out can be very challenging, but from my experience, and the experiences of many people I have known with autism who have moved into supported living houses, moving away from home can be a positive and enriching experience. My only word of advice if you do intend to live at home with family is that since your parents will not be around forever, if they are your primary caregivers and sole means of support then you will need to think about alternative structures for the time when they are no longer able to fulfil that role.

Living with friends or strangers

Living with friends or strangers is one of the most common ways for young or single people to afford to move away from home, and it is no different for those with autism.

The plus side of this living situation is that you are not totally isolated and can receive the often limited social contact that we require, the few minutes of 'good mornings' and 'good evenings' and maybe a few words about the weather up to possibly watching the TV together. If the other members of the household bring friends into the house, it is also a chance to expand your social circle with limited effort and keep the loneliness at bay.

Another benefit of living with neurotypical people is that they can help you through difficult tasks and situations and keep you focused on the activities of everyday living. With the people around you doing the washing up, showering and changing their clothes, it reminds you that perhaps you ought to be doing that too. When bills come in, somebody normally takes charge of this and chases you up for your contribution so you don't have to worry about these things. If something has happened to you during the day that you didn't understand, or someone has said something you're not sure of, there are people on hand to explain it to you or give you advice, to help you fill in a form or phrase a text message. Simply having somebody agree that yes, the milk smells off, or no, that hat doesn't suit you, takes the pressure off you to work everything out for yourself. With supportive and helpful housemates, living with people can have many advantages.

On the other hand, I have never found living with friends or strangers particularly easy, and paradoxically one of the main issues I faced was isolation. Many, if not most, people with autism find socializing very stressful and need to build up to it; furthermore, as mentioned, we often treat our home as a safe place where we can retreat from the pressures of the neurotypical world and recharge our batteries. Living with other people means that we must socialize within our safe haven, allowing us no retreat, and are forced into social situations without warning, without the chance to build up to them, and at odd or inopportune times, which can be terrifying and exhausting. Likewise, even your inner sanctum – your room – does not protect you in this living situation because anybody in the household can knock on your door and demand your attention.

In general, I coped with this by hiding in my room and isolating myself from the other members of the household, sometimes staying silent so that nobody knew if I was home or not. If I wanted to go down to the kitchen to make myself a drink, I knew that I would have to make idle chit-chat as I passed through the living room and think up some excuse not to watch the latest soap opera with them, so would stay in my room and go thirsty. Cooking was a particularly stressful time as it necessitated remaining in the kitchen for up to an hour with sometimes another two people in there, meaning I could not focus on food preparation but had to manoeuvre around others both physically and socially. As a consequence, I often skipped meals, and in the end resorted to keeping tins of tuna, a tin-opener and a fork in my room to sustain myself. In one house that I lived in I memorized everyone's timetables, knowing when I heard the front door close in the afternoon that I had around 15 minutes to use the kitchen and bathroom and get back to my room before another housemate returned from their lecture. Those might be the only 15 minutes of the day I left my room as I found the pressure to make small talk so overwhelming.

A negative consequence of this is that it affects your relationship with your housemates. I found that my isolationist behaviour would result in people knocking on my door and asking if I was okay, inviting me to join them downstairs, offering to make me a coffee, all normal behaviours that for somebody with autism can be anxiety inducing and unwelcome. These would be followed by awkward questions such as, 'Why do you spend so much time in your room?' and 'Don't you like us?' When all that you want is to be left alone to immerse yourself in a book or movie or whatever happens to be your latest obsession, living with people can be frustrating and stressful.

When living with people it is therefore impossible to completely cordon yourself off, and as a result you have to be constantly 'on' and open to the imminent prospect of social communication. Since we spend so much time trying to fit in and act 'normal', home is a place where we like to relax and be ourselves, and having to keep up the act with housemates means we have no time to let out our pent-up autistic behaviours. If you like to initiate social contact on your own terms, at a time of your choosing and in a setting where you can eliminate the stress factors, then living with other people is probably not right for you as you will have little control over such things.

Another issue of living with others is that conflicts will inevitably occur, and we often don't know how to deal with these in appropriate or productive ways. Most of the time when living with people, there will be broadly agreed rules of conduct, such as not leaving your washing up in the sink, rinsing out the bath once you're done with it and following a cleaning rota, and I found that many people fail to uphold these rules as strictly as you might. Furthermore, people can be excessively noisy, and dealing with these situations is not something that most people with autism are naturally good at. Managing conflicts in the public sphere is one thing, but trying to resolve difficulties within your own home is an added level of stress and can often result in tensions within the household, especially as most of us with autism prefer to deal with things bluntly and head on, or conversely not at all and let them simmer.

All in all, living with friends or strangers has its advantages as a means of meeting people and engaging in social contact and is an affordable way of leaving home;

however, it is an often stressful and frustrating manner of living that requires subtle conflict-resolution skills which people with autism don't normally have. Certainly, opening up to your housemates about your autism might be a way of explaining your idiosyncrasies and needs, and if living with friends, they should already have an appreciation of your eccentricities beforehand. Living with strangers is trickier, and it can be a judgement call as to whether you tell them you are on the spectrum. It is often better to be upfront with them from the start, as when moving in with people they are seeing if you're a good fit with them as much as you're seeing if they're a good fit with you, and it is better to know before moving in if there is a compatibility problem, rather than a couple of months down the line. What must be remembered is that all people annoy one another when living together, whether on the autism spectrum or not, and you should enter this living situation with an awareness that you will have to compromise on your needs.

Living alone

Many people that I know with autism opt to live alone as they are unable to cope living with others. It is often more expensive this way and you end up with a smaller space, but the benefits from not having to socialize within your home or share your facilities can make up for the lack of space. It is not difficult to see why living alone is a popular choice for people on the spectrum. With a sturdy front door between you and the world you don't have to answer to anybody who knocks, and you know that other than somebody delivering a parcel, you are unlikely to be disturbed from one day to the next. You can make dinner or drinks any time that you like, without the worry about planning it around somebody else's timetable, and every rule within the household is one that you have come up with and can follow to the letter. Importantly, you do not have to compromise or suppress your autistic behaviours or act a certain way in order to fit in with other people – you can relax and be yourself, provided you follow whatever rules the landlord has in place such as no noise after 11p.m. As a safe retreat from the world, a place to relax and indulge your obsessions as you unwind, I found living alone a far easier, less stressful and more empowering manner of living than sharing with other people.

However, these very benefits can become disadvantages if you're not careful. It is possible to become extremely isolated in this situation, particularly if not working. While many of us might not have friends, and some might not even want them, a certain amount of social contact, such as a simple 'good morning' or 'good evening', is healthy for all of us. Furthermore, if you do want friendships or more social contact, you have to be self-motivating and force yourself out into the community, perhaps joining clubs or accepting invitations from people at work, or even inviting people round. Otherwise, what at first seems great can lead you to become withdrawn, which in turn makes it even harder to socialize. Living alone without working, and with no reason to leave the house except for food shopping, I once spent around three months without talking to anyone. When I then got a job I found I had developed a stutter and shyness that it took me a few years to overcome. I know several people with autism who live alone and find it excruciatingly lonely, yet prefer this to living with people. Unfortunately, there is no ideal solution to this problem and we all must come up with ways of dealing with it.

Another problem with living alone is that in being able to indulge our autistic behaviours without a check, we can lead ourselves into unhealthy lifestyles. When living with people you operate on a regular clock cycle, so that you are aware when it is morning or evening or late at night and alter your behaviour accordingly. For example, when everyone in the household is in bed it's a pretty strong indication that you probably ought to think about going to bed, and when you smell food cooking it reminds you that you need to eat. Living alone, however, you can get out of sync with this regular cycle, especially when dealing with obsessions. As mentioned before, I would often sit down to do a jigsaw puzzle at six in the evening, only to discover to my surprise when I completed it that it was now four in the morning and I hadn't eaten or drunk in ten hours and was due to get up for work soon. Whenever I lived alone I got into unhealthy eating habits, skipping meals for days at a time before binge-eating to compensate, and my sleep pattern revolved around my interests rather than my body's need for rest.

In the long term, unless we are very careful – or employ support workers to help us – living alone can be quite damaging. During the same six months prior to my diagnosis in which I didn't open the post, I also forgot to wash my work clothes; slept through alarms and so was late for work; came home to find I had no food in the freezer; went weeks without shaving; didn't pay bills; missed psychiatric appointments because I hadn't turned over my calendar; and ran out of toilet paper. Needless to say, I lost weight, my physical and mental health declined, my work suffered and my credit rating was damaged. Had I been living with other people, I would not have been allowed to reach this state, but living alone there was nobody to put a stop to it. Without an external check, we can become lost in our obsessions, so I would recommend that anybody with autism who does choose to live alone ensure they have somebody who can come in on a regular basis to safeguard against these self-destructive behaviours.

Living with romantic partners

From the outside, this might not seem like a very comfortable living situation for a person with autism as in a home you share with your significant other there is unlikely to be anywhere that is set aside exclusively for one person. You have to share your kitchen, your bathroom, your bedroom and even your bed, and so the opportunities for shutting yourself off from the social world are few and far between. However, with an understanding partner and a willingness from both parties to compromise, there is no reason that a person with autism cannot live with their partner. Indeed, I have lived with partners both before and after my diagnosis, and I know many people on the spectrum who have successfully managed this living arrangement.

One of the main positives of living with your romantic partner is the joy it can bring. Many people with autism struggle to make friends, often because we cannot tolerate other people or they cannot tolerate us. If we have found someone who not only likes spending time with us but with whom we like spending time too, then we can experience those things that most in the neurotypical world take for granted – love, companionship, shared interests and a sense of acceptance. Socially, we have our best friend within the house so do not become lonely, and practically, we have someone who can help us keep on top of everyday tasks so we do not neglect ourselves. If our partner is neurotypical, they can help us navigate the vagaries of life, and even if they have autism like us, they can still compel us to expand our skillset and do those things we never thought we could. My wife, for example, though she has Asperger's Syndrome too, nags me into making those phone calls that I have been putting off, and encouraged me to become a father, something I had been averse to but which turned out to be one of the best things I've ever done.

However, in order for it to work, certain things must be borne in mind. Communication is essential, more so than in 'normal' relationships, as you and your neurotypical partner might have radically different expectations of what is required from the household, the division of labour and the routines of living. For example, people with autism often fail to notice the housework that needs doing and this can frustrate neurotypical people, so a cleaning rota or explicit instructions on what to do is helpful. Likewise, you might like the routine of eating the same food on the same nights each week, or planning meals long in advance, while your partner might prefer to be spontaneous and have a takeaway meal or go out to a restaurant on a whim if they feel like it. Both partners therefore need to make compromises and 'meet in the middle' to suit everyone.

The partner with autism also needs down time, where they can sit alone and recharge their batteries. If you cannot have your own private place due to lack of space, your neurotypical partner really needs to allow you mental space. I know one person with autism who, when he returns home from work, spends one hour lying on the sofa with his arm over his eyes in total silence before even saying hello to his wife and kids. The whole household accepts that he needs this time to himself after work, and nobody bothers him, and once he has finished he returns to being an active member of the family. Without this, he would become increasingly frustrated and slowly cease to function. The flipside to this, for those of us on the spectrum, is that our partners need time to leave the home and have their own friends and we need similarly to allow this. Many partners with autism cannot understand why their significant other might need other people, and can become jealous and resentful of their partner's greater social success. When our partner goes out with friends, it is an opportunity for us to have our alone time, and we should take advantage of this. In this way, living together can be healthy and mutually beneficial.

Another issue that may need to be faced when living with a partner is a dissimilar need for sleep. Many people with autism have odd sleep patterns, often seeing sleep as an enemy that gets in the way of doing what we want to do. Especially when we work, we can put off going to bed in order to take the time to be ourselves and cater for our hobbies and interests. This is also time we can use to recover our sense of self, calm down, settle ourselves within our minds. I have found in my experience that partners often expect you to go to bed at the same time as them, even if it is a couple of hours earlier than you would naturally, and can become hurt or confused (and feel unloved!) if you regularly stay up into the night or you go to bed with them and then get up later to do something else. However, for many with autism this time is necessary as it is the only alone time we can have on a daily basis. I find that if I do have a series of early nights to please my partner, it creates a negative impact in the long term as I become irritable and tetchy at not having had enough time to unwind. As for neurotypical people with unmatched bedtimes, there is no concrete, easy solution to this problem, though as with everything in a relationship, communication is vital for navigating through it. Explaining why you behave in a certain way, making allowances for one another, perhaps compromising by going to bed early a couple of nights a week, can all make the experience of living together easier.

From the perspective of both the partner with autism and the partner without, the treatment of visitors to the house can cause problems. For the partner with AS or ASD, it is highly likely that there will be more visitors into your home than if you were to live alone, as your partner will doubtless invite round friends and family. Among the people with autism that I know, this is normally met with one of two responses: either you shut yourself away, doing household chores to avoid socializing or simply going somewhere else in the house, or you intrude and dominate the conversation. Both responses can be exasperating to the neurotypical partner as the first can be construed by the visitors as rude while the second means you hog the attention. The best way to deal with this is to ask your partner what is expected of you in these situations. In my household when friends and family of my wife visit, I tend to offer them a drink, sit with them for a little while, and then go and get on with something elsewhere. This way, I have not been rude as I have given them due attention, and I am also giving my wife time alone with her family and friends. Unfortunately, visitors can be very disruptive for those of us with autism – when I go to do something else, I find it difficult to concentrate knowing there are people in my home, and I normally accomplish very little when my wife is entertaining guests. This can be frustrating, but we need to remember that visitors are a normal part of life and the benefits we receive from living with our partners outweigh these negative effects.

The last issue for someone with autism living with a partner is our propensity for becoming attached to objects. At the major level, our obsessions might revolve around collecting, and so our homes can become cluttered, which is not always acceptable to partners. Even if this is not to the point of obsession, it must be addressed at least in part. I can't pass a charity shop without buying a book and so have hundreds, while my wife has thousands of seashells. On a more everyday level, as noted before, people on the spectrum often become attached to individual items of clothing, wearing them even after they have become threadbare and tatty, or display more extreme kinds of hoarding behaviour such as never throwing out newspapers or keeping every receipt they ever receive.

It is difficult to explain to neurotypical people just how difficult it can be for some of us to part with things – they make us feel safe and secure as they are familiar and we like them, and thus we have to sever our emotional bond with them in order to get rid of them, which can be stressful and leave us feeling vulnerable and insecure. However, since a relationship is a partnership, and homes obviously have limited space, it is not fair for one partner to dominate the living spaces with their things. Anybody with autism living with a partner (and by extension anybody whose partner has autism) must be prepared to compromise and meet in the middle. With regard to my household, I have space allocated for my books, and my wife has space allocated for her shells, so as new ones come into the house, old ones have to go to make room for them. These occasions are always gut-wrenching and leave us agitated, but are necessary or else the house would be overflowing (at least, more so than it already is!). My advice to people with autism is to communicate with your partner and come to some arrangement over how much space you can have for your things. Also, tell your partner never to throw anything out without talking to you first: when I first moved in with my wife I threw out some empty plastic juice bottles, since there were 17 in the cupboard, and had not anticipated just how distressed she would become when she found out.

Assisted living

After my diagnosis I was offered a room in an assisted living house for people with autism. This is a service sometimes provided by local autism charities, but if there are none of these in your area, there might be 'halfway houses' provided by other charities for people with mental health difficulties. The idea is that when moving out of your family's home, or when unable to cope entirely by yourself, this is a stepping stone to enable you to live independently in the community with people around to make sure you don't end up in an unhealthy lifestyle by neglecting yourself. Often, they will have sleep-in support workers so that you are able to call on them during the night for assistance and to ensure that house rules are followed so that everybody within the house is comfortable and safe from damaging influences.

I think the choice as to whether to accept a room in an assisted living house is a difficult one. After my last breakdown, living with my parents, I did not have the confidence or wherewithal to move out on my own as it was too big a step; the assisted living house was therefore the perfect environment for me to hone my self-care skills and get some external support in place from care agencies before I could move on and live alone. In this regard, as a means of making people with autism independent of their families and able to function as individuals within the wider community, the safe, protected environment of an assisted living house is very advantageous.

On the other hand, placing four or five people with autism, all of whom have difficulties with social boundaries and communication, under the same roof does not always make for a contented household. I know houses where it works fine and the residents are all friendly; with support they cook meals for one another, socialize together, play games and generally hang out. My experience of living in an assisted living house was rather different. Every time I left my room I had one person who stood too close bombarding me with personal questions while another wanted me to reassure him he was doing the right thing, over and over and over again. People knocked on my door when I clearly did not want to be disturbed; I had to smile constantly or another housemate would think I was cross with him and become upset; and I was on the receiving end of all my own annoying habits. These can be minor, but over time can drag you down – for example, I like the footstool pushed up against the sofa; another person wanted it aligned symmetrically in the centre of the rug. Every time I walked through the lounge I arranged it as I liked it, but I would come back a couple of minutes later to find the footstool had moved as if by magic. It was daily passive-aggressive torture. Sometimes I felt like we were being secretly filmed for a crazy reality TV show. While it was a good way of becoming independent, and I would recommend it as a stepping stone, living in the assisted living house was a frustrating and bewildering experience.

I would, however, definitely caution against living in a house for people with mental health difficulties. One of the residents in my house when I first moved in was given to sudden violent outbursts and generally aggressive behaviour; this made the house an unsafe place and made me fearful to leave my room, which is the opposite of what these houses are designed for. It set me back quite a way as it knocked my confidence and I visited my parents daily to escape; he was eventually evicted after making threats to kill. I know another person with autism who moved out of his safe home with his parents and was placed in a house with a schizophrenic and a manic-depressive; with violence and shouting, he similarly locked himself in his room, didn't eat, became very fearful and depressed, and ended up back at home with his parents. The idea behind assisted living houses is good, but the reality can be something very different and living with people with behavioural problems can often create more problems than it solves.

Moving home
Other than the death of a loved one and divorce, moving house is commonly reckoned to be the most stressful thing

a person can do in life. It disrupts your routine, you have to sever your attachment to a home whether you liked the place or not, it forces you to sort through your belongings and either pack them or get rid of them, it stirs up emotions through memories of good and bad times, and provokes doubt that you're doing the right thing and fear of the new situation you find yourself in. This can be even harder if the move is one that is being forced on you and you are moving to a place you do not actually wish to inhabit. And that is for people without an Autism Spectrum Disorder.

If we add autism into the mix, it is clear that moving house directly affects the very things most of us depend on to function: stability, comfortable routines and a familiar safe haven filled with our belongings. For someone with autism, moving home can therefore be excruciating. Unfortunately, given that our condition often leads to an unstable work life and turbulent sexual relationships, we can often find ourselves having to move frequently throughout our lives. In the ten years between turning 18 and being diagnosed with Asperger's Syndrome at 28, I moved home ten times, while after my diagnosis I have moved home five times. From these moves, and those of people I know with autism, I have learned it is vitally important to ensure there are adequate support structures in place both during and after the move, and I would strongly recommend against moving away from family and friends.

Even with support structures in place, it is impossible to eradicate some of the negative effects of a move and thus it is never an easy experience for a person on the spectrum. No matter how quickly you unpack and re-establish your routine, it has been my experience, and that of others I know with autism, that moving home leaves you fundamentally unsettled for some time, ranging from a few weeks to a few months. It is an all-pervading sense that things are not right with the world and though you cannot put your finger on why, something feels wrong. I always feel oddly vulnerable after a move, and despite making sure the doors and windows are locked and the smoke alarm works, nothing can allay this irrational sense of being exposed and open to attack. Anybody with autism considering a move needs to be aware that it takes time for these feelings to go away and a sense of routine, comfort and safety to return. I say this not to put anybody with autism off moving home, but to reassure them that while you will feel out of sorts for a time, and will likely be terrified on occasion (I find myself hiding under tables and in cupboards whenever I move), it will pass, a sense of normalcy will return, and ultimately the new place will become your safe haven if you allow it to.

SUMMARY

- Many adults with high-functioning autism live at home with their parents.
- Most Aspies treat home as a safe place where we can retreat from the social world, hoard our belongings and indulge our obsessions.
- It can be stressful living with friends, strangers or partners.
- You must be careful not to become too isolated or obsessed with your hobbies.
- If you do not have physical space, it is important to build some 'mental space' into your daily routine.

CHAPTER 6

Autism in the Workplace

Some people with high-functioning autism have never worked and will never work, as their particular idiosyncrasies keep them from gainful employment. Others, like me, might have bounced from job to job with gaps in-between as we struggled to cope in a neurotypical work environment without a diagnosis. And there are some who will have worked steadily throughout their lives and for whom the diagnosis of autism changes nothing. For some people on the spectrum, work can be an intolerable nightmare, while for others it is something that they enjoy and benefit from. The point is that having autism does not preclude you from work, but nor does it mean that all people with autism can or should work. The sad truth is that while most of us with AS or ASD are intellectually capable of working, we often cannot meet the social requirements that are never included on the job application but are actually a key aspect of the role.

The working world, already a stressful place, can be even more stressful for someone with autism. Before my diagnosis I had numerous jobs, working in office administration, retail, nursing, reception, secretarial, telesales and the police, and while working I found it impossible to create a healthy work–life balance or indeed cope with the pressures of both doing the job and fitting into the work environment. I have never had a job that I did not dread going into and that did not adversely affect my mental health, leading to several breakdowns, depression, anxiety and self-harm. Every morning I would arrive 15 minutes early, sit in my car and psyche myself up to go in, paint on a happy face, act normal, act natural, I can do this, lock myself in the bathroom if I was having a panic attack, sit in my car at lunch and try to build up my confidence and self-esteem to return and face the afternoon, and then worry all evening about having to do it all over again the following day. Clearly, I am capable of doing many kinds of job; however, I cannot guarantee that if I took those jobs, I would not be a neurotic, suicidal mess a couple of months down the line. Therefore, I think that while having a job boosts self-esteem and helps a person on the autism spectrum feel an active part of society, you need to think very carefully before entering a situation you might not be able to handle and should never allow someone to pressurize you into taking an inappropriate job role. It is up to each individual with autism whether we feel ready or able to work, and where and how we wish to work, and it is not for others to stigmatize those who cannot work, or make us feel like a burden to society. We all give back where and when we can.

Types of job
The types of job taken by people at the high-functioning end of the autism spectrum are as diverse as the individuals with the condition. There are rock stars, actors, singers, authors, sports stars, economists, film directors, comedians, businessmen and politicians with the condition who have gone far in their chosen professions. Many people with autism work in teaching and academia, computing,

accounting, engineering and medicine, while others prefer to work in shops or garages, customer services or office administration. I know someone with autism who works as a pest controller and another who is a gardener, so really there is no 'typical' job for an Aspie.

That said, there are certain key characteristics that many with autism find useful in their careers. Routine is an important feature, particularly when combined with an organizing or arranging principle, and while I like to think of myself as an exciting, spontaneous person, the reality is that my least-hated job was data entry, typing lists of numbers into spreadsheets for eight hours a day, because it was repetitive and rhythmic, and I didn't have to talk to people. I know people with autism who work as postmen as they enjoy sorting the post and doing the same route every day. At a smaller level, it can help to have a routine in whatever job you do, whether it is the words you use when you answer the phone, the manner in which you deal with a customer, or the way you organize your tasks for the day. These routines can help you feel in control, significantly improving your enjoyment of the role.

Obsessiveness is another feature of autism that you can use to benefit your work. Academia and computer programming are two obvious examples where an obsessive interest in a narrow field enhances career prospects, while I've met many tour guides who are probably on the autism spectrum. Working in specialist subject areas that require you to memorize facts can be similarly rewarding. As a medical secretary working on a thoracic medicine ward I learned all of the terminology related to the field and how to spell it, so that I was able to clear a six-month backlog of audio typing in a month. After that, I was transferred around the hospital from department to department to clear their backlogs, necessitating learning entirely new medical terms every few weeks, which I excelled at. It probably also helped that, as an audio typist, I sat in an office by myself and didn't have to deal with people.

Ultimately, as with most things, success in a job is about minimizing the negative aspects of your condition and maximizing the positive, and it is up to you to work out what you do well and what you don't. For example, eccentricity is tolerated and sometimes openly encouraged among college lecturers or the creative arts, but not in lawyers or hotel receptionists. Many people with autism prefer to deal with things, such as facts and figures and organizing, than with people, and so would be better working in office administration than social care. Some are much better at dealing with people over the telephone than face to face and so work in customer services, while others struggle with short-term memory and become easily distracted, so wouldn't cope on a till sorting out change for customers. The jobs I have found most difficult were those without clear guidelines, where you had to use 'common sense' when dealing with people, such as working as a care assistant. Many people with autism feel their ideal job would be working from home, and if possible, this is certainly something I'd recommend. We can have successful careers, but only if we discover how best to incorporate our autism into our working life.

Routine working

Because of a love of routines and commitment to following rules, many people with autism approach our work systematically, completing each step before moving onto the next, and so on until the task is finished. Thanks to this trait, we are often very punctual, reliable and hardworking. However, this systematic approach to work can make it difficult to multitask, starting one job, leaving it half-finished to start something else, then going back to the original job, and so forth. Work often requires us to multitask to a greater or lesser extent, prioritizing tasks and parts of tasks, and this is something that I have always struggled with. Furthermore, it can be difficult to grasp the concept of an open-ended task, since many of us with autism work best with a series of steps, an end goal and clearly defined parameters.

Another issue with systematic work is that people on the spectrum often don't have the flexibility to make changes to these systems or routines in situations where they don't work. As an example, when I worked in a police control room I received a call from an 11-year-old boy to say he'd kicked his ball over the fence and the neighbour was refusing to give it back. Although I knew it was a stupid call and that my colleagues would ridicule me if I took a crime report, I had been trained to take a crime report in cases of theft. As I went through the process, systematically making out the report as I usually did, I desperately tried to think of a way out of it, but couldn't. When I transmitted the report, I was, as I had expected, roundly criticized and told to use common sense in future. However, I never managed to figure out how to use 'common sense' to avoid taking silly crime reports when, moving step by step, there was to my mind no point in the process where I could stop.

Related to our often routine method of working, many people with autism are perfectionists, a symptom of black-and-white, all-or-nothing thinking. We work at a job until it is not only finished but finished to the best of our abilities; we want everything to be 'just so', and are fastidious that everything is in the right place, every 't' crossed and every 'i' dotted. While on the one hand this is a plus, since it leads to a very high quality of work, it can have a detrimental effect on our output and cause added stress. In work situations, instead of work being done to the highest possible standard, it often needs to be rushed through in order to meet a deadline. Furthermore, sometimes you need to be able to stop what you're doing at the end of your shift, 'down tools' and go home, leaving the task unfinished until the morning. Unfortunately, this perfectionism also means that we can be annoyed with people who do not share our same lofty ideals, and short with those who bring down the quality of our work.

Social exhaustion

Most of us diagnosed with autism as adults will be experts at masking our condition by imitating the behaviour of our more socially successful peers and compensating for our lack of intuitive awareness by conscious processing. What neurotypical people often just instinctively 'get', we generally have to expend a great deal of mental effort figuring out. In the jobs I have done, if I have an eight-hour shift, I will spend the entire time trying to work out the social rules of the work environment, watching what I say, how I sit, the way I look at people, trying to interpret what they say and how they say it, making sure I'm not too close to people or too far away, that my voice is at an appropriate volume, that I say the right things, that I'm making the right amount of eye contact, and working out whether someone is joking or being serious, or if I should join in the gossip about person A, or if I can reveal what I know about person B without it being a betrayal of trust – and that is on top of doing the job that I am paid for. Indeed, for every eight-hour shift I spend at work, it feels like I have worked 16 hours – eight doing the job, and eight trying to cope with the social aspects of the situation. On a 12-hour shift, it can feel like 24 hours of effort.

Nor does it end when the shift is over. Upon going home, I run through the events of the day, the conversations, the situations, and analyse them and process them and mine them for whatever information I can use to make the social aspects of the next shift that little bit easier. This is, quite obviously, physically, mentally and emotionally exhausting. As a result of the greater amount of mental processing, people with autism can tire more quickly than neurotypical people, and the same amount of time working can have a much greater negative impact on our home life as we have no energy left in the evening to do those things that help us relax. The next day, we do it again, and the next, and the next, with ever-depleting energy levels, until our lives revolve around work and recovering from work. People with autism are therefore often exhausted as a result of the social aspects of the work environment, and this is something that you should be aware of.

Dealing with authority

Given our penchant for accuracy, efficiency and loyalty, one would imagine an employee with AS or ASD would be a manager's dream. However, our relationships with bosses or other authority figures can sometimes be strained for a variety of reasons. Many people with autism can struggle to understand the different registers for speaking to different people, in that the lunch room banter with your co-worker is rarely an appropriate way of talking to the managing director, who might be offended by the informality with which you address him or her. Conversely, people with autism can be timid and shy around authority figures – whenever I worked with doctors as a nursing assistant, medical secretary or doctor's receptionist, I was irrationally fearful of them, treating them with undue amounts of deference and even stuttering in their presence.

Three common features of people with autism can also cause problems: honesty, fairness and commitment to accuracy. To get on with your boss, sometimes honesty is not the best policy, but many of us cannot bend the truth simply to please our employer. I was once asked by a manager before a meeting with the finance department to pretend I had left the figures on my desk – I was unable to do this as I had the figures with me. Similarly, people on the spectrum are often very fair-minded, and if the boss acts in a way that you deem to be unfair, it can provoke quite negative feelings and reactions. If I have worked really hard at something and somebody else has put in little effort, yet we both receive the same amount of praise, I can quickly feel underappreciated. Likewise, if in front of his boss a manager tries to blame the team for his own mistakes, I will stand up for the team, which does not make one a popular employee.

Related to this, people with autism can get into trouble with authority for our tactless commitment to accuracy. When I was a child, I pointed out my teachers' spelling mistakes to them, not to belittle them or humiliate them by being corrected by a six-year-old, but because they were inaccurate. I still have not learned when it is imprudent to point out your superior's mistakes. For example, I had a boss who asked me if I'd done the report he'd asked for. I told him he hadn't asked me for a report. He said he'd e-mailed me about it. He hadn't, so not only was he being inaccurate, he was being unfair. I told him he hadn't e-mailed me. He assured me that he had. I told him that he most certainly hadn't. Becoming angry, he told me that he most certainly had. And so it went on. The 'appropriate' way to have dealt with this would have been to apologize for missing his e-mail and tactfully ask him to resend it, whereupon he may have realized, as he looked at his computer, that he had not actually sent it.

Instead, knowing that I was right and he was wrong, I did not concede the point, which escalated the exchange into a head-to-head.

Like many people with autism, I have difficulty exploring alternative ways of doing things or understanding the seemingly nonsensical needs of other people. If you have a certain way of doing things, in a certain sequence, it is because that is how you understand it and because to you, this is and will always be the 'right' way of doing it. This can bring people with autism up against our bosses who want us to do things in a different way that we can only see as being the 'wrong' way of doing it. While our insistence that we're always right might be annoying to others in a social context, in an employer–employee relationship we have to learn the ability to back down, as our employer's authority overrides our insistence that our way is the best and only way. Rigidity of thinking, a lack of tact, and a commitment to honesty, accuracy and fairness means that people on the autism spectrum can often have adversarial relationships with their managers. While it is clearly not advisable to antagonize the person who conducts your appraisal, many of us are simply unable to 'play the game', and this can have a negative impact on career progression and financial rewards.

Relationships with co-workers

Unfortunately work, as with the rest of life, is a social environment that is filled with unwritten rules. Many of us with autism struggle to understand how we are supposed to act in a work environment. You are meant to have a certain amount of small talk or chit-chat with your colleagues to break down barriers, build trust and foment a positive working relationship, but many people on the spectrum find this incredibly difficult or even pointless. The tendency can be to raise inappropriate or complex subjects for discussion, which, instead of easing relations with others, actually strains them. For example, when I was working in a hospital, I would try to engage my colleagues in discussions about the medico-legal issues surrounding abortion or euthanasia, while they preferred to gossip about the latest reality TV show and simply wanted to get through to the end of the shift. Since each environment we enter has slightly different rules about what is appropriate, the level of formality, how we address people at different positions within the hierarchy, many of us on the autism spectrum can feel like we are walking through a minefield, not knowing which way to turn or how to behave, which has a negative impact on our relationships with our colleagues.

Many of the issues we can have with our co-workers stem from a combination of difficulties understanding social rules and the fact that people with autism are generally task-oriented people. When a co-worker returns from holiday you are supposed to ask them about it, comment on their tan, discuss how the weather there compared with back home, and so on. I knew a lady with AS who instead immediately told people what work they had missed and how much they needed to catch up on. In a work setting, she was, quite logically, focused on the task she was employed to do, not making friends in a social setting. Because of this, we can run roughshod over people's feelings, particularly if they're doing things wrong. I worked with a woman who had been in her position for years and was very popular, but made many mistakes with simple administrative tasks. The others in the office would quietly correct her mistakes in a spirit of *bonhomie*; I would point out to her that she was making mistakes, and this is how we've all been trained to do it, so please do it that way in future. This lack of attention to people's feelings when they hinder the goal or task that we're performing is a very common feature of autism.

What makes it even more difficult to form positive relationships with our colleagues is that many of them rely on social events organized in and around work, which those of us on the spectrum can find very stressful. Going out for drinks at lunch, the Christmas party, a meal for someone's leaving do, are all part of 'getting on' in a job. If you attend training courses and are put up in a hotel, it is expected that you socialize with your work colleagues in the evening, and this puts added pressure on those of us who find these social situations excruciating. No matter how well you have learned the 'rules' of the workplace, as soon as you enter these social situations the rules change regarding what you can talk about and how you are supposed to act. My solution tends to be to avoid such social situations, but that is often viewed negatively by work colleagues, and can be a risky strategy because I have found that work social situations involve a horrendous amount of time gossiping about or even badmouthing co-workers. Indeed, when working in an office I felt pressured to attend these events as it gave people less opportunity to talk about me behind my back.

Office politics is something that greatly complicates matters for those of us with autism who already struggle to negotiate relationships with work colleagues. In virtually every work environment there are rivalries, personality conflicts and differences of opinion between people that range from the petty to the quite serious, and can draw others into difficult situations. Oftentimes, either party to the conflict will attempt to influence you one way or the other and recruit you to their 'side'. Since this particular aspect of work life is based on manipulation and secrecy, often employing indirect, passive-aggressive tactics instead of open, outright confrontation, people with autism are poorly equipped to deal with it, especially if they're on the receiving end.

Our difficulty forming positive work relationships can have a damaging effect on our long-term career prospects. Getting on in a job has as much to do with understanding the social rules of the workplace as it does with doing the actual tasks you're employed to do, and sometimes the two can be one and the same thing. In many large companies, in order to carry out your job you may need cooperation from people in various different departments who are under no obligation to assist you ahead of others, and so an ability to form relationships with people in other parts of the business, known in management speak as 'networking', is often a prerequisite. It is also true that successful networking and an ability to get on with others are two key factors in being considered for promotion, particularly to management level. Since we are often unable to form these relationships due to our autism, we can be at a disadvantage from the very start.

The unfortunate truth I realized in all the jobs I worked in was that no matter how hard I tried to mask my condition, and no matter how much effort I put in to learn the social rules and keep things positive and functional, it was virtually inevitable that because of my autism I would commit a multitude of social gaffes. It can be heartbreaking to have tried so hard to get it right, and suddenly say something and discover you have become a pariah. For example, after 11 months in a job forming what I felt to be positive working relationships, I congratulated a popular colleague on getting 'knocked up'. At the time, this was the title of a popular movie and I thought it was simply another term for being pregnant. Apparently, this term was offensive, particularly as my colleague had been having fertility treatment. It spread around the office, and before I knew it I was ostracized and I had no idea why until my manger took me to one side and told me he was going to have to discipline me. To this day, I still do not understand the furore around this event. However, this was before my diagnosis with Asperger's Syndrome, and I would like to think that should the same thing happen today, I would be given the benefit of the doubt if I explained that I had meant no offence.

Bullying

Bullying is a word that is overused these days, but is unfortunately a real aspect of the working world. People with AS and ASD are all too commonly bullied in the workplace, and it is rare to find a person diagnosed as an adult who has not experienced this at some point. Having autism makes us an easy target for bullies as we are different, don't know how to fight back and don't know how to cope with the situation, and the bullies can see that. I have often been ostracized at work, and this isn't helped by the social gaffes I made without even knowing it. When I was once asked to put money in a collection for the birthday of a person I'd never met, I refused as I'd never met them; despite my having put money in numerous other birthday collections, the rumour was spread that I was a 'miser', and so for my birthday there was no collection. Similarly, if I was at a table with six people, someone would go round and individually invite each of the others to a party in front of me, but pointedly ignore me. The same happened with Christmas cards, or making drinks for people – a work environment can sometimes feel like being back at school.

The bullying can take a more active form. When I was working at the police, the sergeant would frequently put me down in front of my colleagues, even shouting and swearing at me across the control room. Not sure how to deal with it, after ten months of this behaviour I eventually told him where to go, but in such a manner that I was again disciplined, even though my boss acknowledged that the sergeant was a bully and I had been provoked. In one job, people said things about me so that they would be given the nice shifts and lunch breaks while I got the nasty shifts and poorly timed breaks. In another job, people seemed to think that if anything went wrong, they could shift the blame onto me as they knew nobody would stick up for me. I do wonder if the reaction to my 'knocked up' comment was less about the offensiveness of the comment itself and more about people deliberately stirring it up to provoke a reaction.

Attitudes to autism, work and welfare

As discussed in Chapter 2, disclosing your condition to your employer or co-workers does not make you immune to prejudice and it does not eliminate the difficulties of the workplace. I worked with a man with AS who had the habit of speaking at a volume too loud to be comfortable about topics that really weren't appropriate for the workplace. Everyone knew he had autism, but it did not stop people making fun of him behind his back, making quite nasty comments to his face, and ultimately setting him up to fail until he was forced out of the job. Of course, if someone is disruptive in the workplace, it is up to their supervisors to counsel them towards a more appropriate manner of behaving; however, allowances need to be made for people who don't have an awareness that they speak too loudly, and people can be markedly intolerant even when they know the person can't help it. I have heard people say that those with autism should be made to work as cleaners or collect trolleys at supermarkets as 'the workplace is not a day care centre'. We are all different, and the idea that everyone with autism should work as a cleaner or trolley collector is clearly inappropriate.

Attitudes can be even worse if you are unable to work because of your condition but appear outwardly 'normal'. This is true for AS and ASD along with wider mental health problems, since visible, long-term physical ailments tend to receive more sympathy among the public than those that are hidden. With the issue of benefits and welfare being a flash point, there is a stigma against people who are on long-term sickness or otherwise out of work. While some people certainly use state handouts to avoid working, those who are genuinely unable to work are often erroneously perceived as workshy, lazy and greedy. In periods when I have not been working, I have faced open hostility from both acquaintances and strangers alike, and indeed these attacks can be quite personal, with negative judgements made about your character. I have been told many times when I have not been working that I am 'lucky' to have an 'excuse' like Asperger's Syndrome and that I have an 'easy life'. Anybody who has read this book should be able to see that living with autism is certainly not 'easy', and nor would I describe someone with the condition as 'lucky' compared with someone without it. I think life is equally hard for everybody, and until you have walked a mile in someone's shoes you should not judge them. As long as you know that you are genuinely unable to work then it really does not matter what other people think. It is often not worth the bother of defending yourself since if someone has made up their mind that you do not work because you are simply lazy then no explanation about how going to work causes you to have anxiety, self-harming behaviour, mental breakdowns and increased risk of suicide will change it.

Accommodating your needs

If you do decide to disclose your autism to your employers, it is important to think about what you would like from them in order to better fulfil your job role and ease the mental strain caused by your condition. For some people on the spectrum, you might require nothing at all. Looking back over my work life, however, I think there are many small adjustments that could have made a world of difference to me and cost my employers nothing. The most important thing I could have asked of an employer if I had known I had autism was to mediate for me with co-workers when there was a misunderstanding. Conflict resolution is something most of us with autism struggle with, and so a helping hand to diffuse workplace disagreements would have been very useful. Furthermore, somebody to keep an eye on me to ensure that I was not bullied, ostracized or isolated as a result of my autism could have been of great utility. In particular, you might consider requesting your employers provide you with a mentor – a co-worker, perhaps, or your manager – who could operate as a single point of contact for advice on social and communication matters that might arise during your day-to-day work.

You could also request clear guidelines for workplace behaviour, and comprehensive instructions for carrying out specific tasks. While an employer might feel it patronizing to be explicit about how something is to be carried out, since people with autism often take things literally and struggle with so-called 'common sense', the more detailed the instructions, especially if they are written down instead of spoken, the less chance of misinterpretations or mistakes. Before my diagnosis I worked in a residential care home and was asked one morning to give Mr X a bath. He had suffered a stroke and was paralysed down one side and unable to communicate, so I duly collected him from his room, bathed him and returned him to his room before moving onto my next assigned task. I was later reprimanded by the manager with the words, 'You left a man in a wheelchair in a dressing gown all morning. Use more common sense in future.' I spent the rest of the day wondering which chair I should have put him in if I wasn't supposed to leave him in his wheelchair all morning, and it wasn't until I got home that night that I realized she was talking about the *dressing gown* – I should have dressed him when we got back to the room! Since I had been instructed to bathe him, I did so – it didn't even occur to me to dress him afterwards. While at the time I was mortified at making such an obvious mistake, looking back it seems plain that this was a result of my autism. Clear instructions on what was expected of me would have avoided this mistake.

As another example of how simple it is to address an autistic need, when I worked on the telephone at the police we wore headsets with only one earpiece. This meant that when I was on a call my uncovered ear could hear all the other conversations going on around me, which I found incredibly distracting and made it difficult to focus on my job. I was therefore allocated a headset with two earpieces – and this was before my diagnosis. Really, the accommodations that you request are up to you, based on how your autism affects you, but you have to be realistic about the changes an employer can make. If you are seen to get preferential treatment, it can further damage your relationship with co-workers and, of course, if everybody has to change their manner of working to accommodate you, it might indicate that you are in the wrong job role.

SUMMARY

- People with high-functioning autism can work in all kinds of fields.

- We often like jobs that prioritize routine and accuracy, but our all-or-nothing approach can cause us stress.

- While most people with AS and ASD are physically able to do a job, we often struggle to do it because of the social aspects of the workplace.

- People with autism are very susceptible to workplace bullying and often have difficulties 'getting along' with co-workers and employers.

- We can find work mentally exhausting and often find it hard to create a healthy work–life balance.

- Think hard about what could make your work life easier.

CHAPTER 7

Social and Romantic Relationships

Since the cornerstones of forming relationships are social communication, social interaction and social imagination, the same three principal areas affected by autism, many of us have difficulties in this area. You might have been told that people with autism do not want social or romantic relationships, but this is a myth. While it is true that many of us struggle to create or maintain them, this does not mean that we do not want them. I have met some people with autism who, as a result of their experiences of repeated failure, have decided not to pursue friendships or relationships and focus on spending their lives on their own, but this is a rarity. Most people with autism have the same social and sexual needs and desires as any member of society. Unfortunately, given our handicap with forming relationships, this means that there are many in the autism community who are desperately lonely. Equally, there are some, such as myself, who are married with children, and others who are quite popular. Therefore, please feel reassured that having autism does not preclude the possibility of making friends or having long-term, meaningful relationships – it simply makes it harder to form and keep them, but when you find one that works, it makes it all the more special.

This chapter, as should be clear, covers how your autism might affect your friendships and relationships. It is not a guide to making friends or attracting romantic partners, but there are plenty of books and websites out there for that. However, along with exposing some of the issues faced in this area by those on the autism spectrum, this chapter does contain some advice and tips from experience. I have grouped social and romantic relationships together in a single chapter because they share many of the same features, and the way autism affects our approach to friendships and romantic relationships can be markedly similar. As always, different people have different approaches and their autism affects them in different ways. Likewise, no two friendships or relationships will be the same, and different people can handle different levels of social stimulation than others. The key is finding out what works for you. I, for example, only need one close friend or partner to meet my social needs. My wife, on the other hand, has lots of friends and acquaintances and needs constant contact with a wide variety of people to meet her social needs. How your autism affects this area of your life therefore depends on you.

General characteristics

Generally speaking, people at the high-functioning end of the autism spectrum understand social and romantic relationships from an intellectual viewpoint rather than an intuitive or emotional one. Essentially, while a neurotypical person will be guided by their heart and what feels natural, those of us with AS or ASD often try to think, or overthink, our way into and through relationships. Lacking the social understanding that people seem to develop as they grow up, and thanks to our black-and-white thinking, we latch onto the extraneous, obvious features of relationships without appreciating their deeper significance. For example, when asked what we understand by 'friendship', most people I have met with autism describe a reciprocal supply-and-demand type of relationship, in that you become friends with somebody so they have someone to go fishing with and you have someone to go to the movies with, or you can help them put up a shelf while they can help you erect a fence. The deeper understanding of friendships fulfilling complex emotional and social needs, as opposed to practical ones, can be missing. We also find it difficult to understand or conceive of another person's wants and desires, and so can be perfectly happy in a friendship without realizing the other person feels neglected or used.

We can have a similarly different understanding of romantic relationships. People with autism can think that the only difference between a romantic relationship and a friendship is that in the former, you have sex. This makes sense from a purely quantitative view, but it misses the point that sexual relationships are meant to be deeper, more intimate and emotional, than friendships. We can fail to understand that the other person wants us to ask how their day was, and to make them feel special and significant, and all the things that neurotypical people often expect as a matter of course. We often don't spontaneously share our thoughts, experiences and emotions with the other person as is common in a romantic relationship, and can come across as careless of the other person's needs. It is not that we dismiss the other person's needs – it is that sometimes we aren't even aware that they *have* needs, and so are blissfully unaware that we are omitting to do something. Furthermore, we think that loving someone is enough, and don't realize we have to outwardly demonstrate that love. For example, I found with my girlfriends, and now with my wife, that women in relationships require occasional 'love tokens' in the form of gifts of flowers or love notes to emphasize that you love them. From an intellectual point of view, I struggle to understand how spending money on flowers that will be dead in a few days is more an expression of love than the fact that I'm married to her, but such outward demonstrations are something we can learn how to do.

While we try to *understand* relationships intellectually, this does not mean that people with autism approach them unemotionally, however. We feel them just as deeply, and appreciate them just as much, as neurotypical people. Some might argue we are incapable of genuinely loving another person, but it is very difficult to categorize what love is and therefore whether those feelings are 'genuinely' love or not. Certainly, like anybody, we long for friendships and romantic relationships, are troubled when they don't work, miss people when they are gone, want to please them, and are anxious about doing the wrong things. We want to be good friends and partners and can, in fact, place too much emphasis on relationships. Many with autism idealize the concept, learning about it from books, television and movies and building it up into something with which reality cannot compete. Similarly, many of us have a fairy-tale concept of love and romantic relationships, seeking a perfect soulmate who can make everything better and fulfil all our emotional, social and physical needs so that we can live happily ever after. Alternatively, we might have learned about relationships from soap operas and feel that they are meant to be unstable, dramatic affairs that bounce from crisis to crisis so that we can reaffirm our love for one another. Since we might lack a genuine understanding of what a sexual relationship is, we can turn them into a charade of what we think they ought to be instead of what they actually are. It is, therefore, no surprise that our relationships with both neurotypicals and Aspies themselves can be difficult since we all have different understandings and expectations of what is required.

Boundaries

Closely related to the above, most people with autism like clear boundaries, definable structures and concrete rules. Unfortunately, neither friendships nor romantic relationships come with manuals for anybody, neurotypical, autistic or otherwise. We often have to 'feel' our way into relationships, whether friendly or romantic, moving slowly and subtly, in small steps and tiny incremental stages. They are intuitive, tacitly negotiated without ever being explicitly discussed, can last a few days to a lifetime, can be very intense very quickly or never get beyond a passing acquaintance, and are governed by rules and conventions that people naturally pick up as they grow and develop. Therefore, they rely upon skills that those of us with autism do not naturally possess and that run counter to everything we are good at.

Whether it is a friendship or romantic relationship, I have found most people on the spectrum, myself included, are very anxious about defining or categorizing our relationships. People I know with autism often ask me the nature of our association – are we friends? What type of friends are we? They are obviously fishing for some manner of definition whereby they can understand the rules of our interaction – what they should and shouldn't say, the level of formality and the amount of emotional attachment. Another example is worrying about the point where a friendship becomes a relationship. If you go on a date with somebody and you agree to meet up again, does this mean that they are your girlfriend or just an acquaintance? There is also, I must admit, a fair deal of paranoia when you seem to be forming a relationship with someone. You find yourself tempted to ask them if they like you, why they want to be friends with you, because you are unable to understand for yourself what is going on. I often wonder if people actually like me or if they have an ulterior motive of some kind. None of these concerns, it must be pointed out, are exclusive to autism, and many people without the condition experience the same worries and insecurities; however, if you are on the spectrum, you are likely to experience these sensations.

Unfortunately, as a result of our autism we often get things wrong and can scare away the other person and irreparably harm the relationship in its early stages. It is quite common for someone with autism to come on too strong too soon because we assume we have become friends with somebody and bombard them with compliments and invitations to events and want to hang out with them and discuss personal, intimate topics, only to discover they were only ever an acquaintance and now they think we're weird. Alternatively, we can take things too slowly, not realizing the depth of the relationship we have formed, and can remain aloof and standoffish as we think we are not yet at that stage, which can equally damage the association with the other person as they think we are not interested. In romantic relationships, we can be very uncertain about the rate at which the partnership is moving, and instead of letting things happen 'naturally' will try to work to a specific and arbitrary timescale of when we think things should happen. This puts pressure on the relationship, and the other person, and it is our very desire not to mess things up that means we do.

A related difficulty for people with autism is not being able to distinguish between liking somebody as a friend and liking them due to a physical or romantic attraction. When I was single, if I met somebody that I liked and they seemed to like me, I often became confused about what it was I liked about them, and tried to analyse the feelings I was having and the nature of our association to work out what I wanted from the relationship. Since emotions can be confusing, and our understanding of social situations is patchy at best, I would often misconstrue an overture of friendship as somebody making a pass at me, and respond accordingly, to the detriment of the relationship. People with autism are therefore often unable to navigate this fine line between friendship and romantic attraction, leading us to lose perfectly fine friendships, which we made awkward by mistaking them for something more.

In Chapter 3 I mentioned a traffic light analogy that a psychotherapist used to explain to me that, just as the lights have an amber between red and green, friendships and relationships do not go from nothing to everything in a single stage. This certainly helped me understand that I needed to allow relationships to evolve naturally, step by step, without forcing them or trying to artificially create something that was not there. I think all people with AS or ASD should bear this in mind when thinking about friendships and relationships, to remind themselves that we need to allow them to grow. Similarly, it is useful to remember that friendships and relationships involve two people, so it is not down to us to control the evolution of the relationship, nor are we the only ones who need to suggest activities and topics of conversation – we can equally allow the more experienced social or sexual partner to guide us into the friendship or relationship without the pressure being on us to turn it into something that we don't actually understand.

All or nothing

Another issue people with autism can have with forming and keeping relationships is a black-and-white, all-or-nothing approach. In friendships, we can often want to be the very best of friends or not at all; in romantic relationships, we want to be your best friend, lover, soulmate, partner, confidant, bedrock, comforter, parent and child, or otherwise not be with you. Because of this approach, it can be difficult for us to maintain more than one relationship at a time. For example, I am only capable of having either a close friendship or a romantic relationship, never both at the same time. I find it too difficult to divide my attention, thoughts and energies between two separate people, or consider the needs of more than one other person at a time. Furthermore, I often feel as though I am betraying my partner if I am socially interested in another person. Of course, it is entirely normal and natural to have a number of friends in addition to your romantic partner, and you are allowed to be emotionally attached to them, but it is not something that I am able to do and that is just something I have had to accept.

An unfortunate side-effect of having an all-or-nothing approach to relationships, even if you are able to have multiple friends, is that it places a lot of pressure on your partner and can cause instability in romantic relationships. The other person can feel smothered by having you focus your attention exclusively on them, expecting them to meet all your needs and boost your self-esteem and do everything with you. For example, if I want to go to the movies, I want to go with my wife and I want to talk about the things I'm interested in; however, it is highly unusual that you will ever find anybody who is into exactly the same things as you, and we have different tastes in movies and want to talk about different things. This is normal and fine when each partner has other friends with whom they can see these movies or talk about these topics, but if all you have is the other person, not all of your social needs are met. It can also be awkward when you argue with your partner, for the very person you go to for comfort and advice is the one person you can't go to in that situation.

At its extreme, the all-or-nothing approach means that people on the autism spectrum are prone to co-dependency and obsession. It can be very easy for our friends or partners to become the object around which our lives revolve and the people who give us a sense of security and self-worth. People with autism can be particularly clingy, wanting to spend all our time with our significant other, resenting spending time alone, not understanding why the other person wants space, and even subordinating our own interests and needs in order to please the other person. Many people with autism similarly think they need to 'reward' the other person for liking them, showering them with endless presents in an attempt to buy their friendship or doing tasks for them to make themselves indispensable. In the long term, these behaviours can be damaging not only to the relationships but to the individuals themselves, for the person with autism becomes entirely dependent on the other for their self-esteem and self-worth, which is very unhealthy, especially if and when the relationship ends. As with my wife being my only friend, an all-or-nothing approach to relationships does not necessarily have to be a bad thing if it meets your social needs and does not impinge upon your partner's freedom, but people with autism must be very careful to avoid obsession.

Exploitation

People with autism are often inexperienced, naïve and gullible, and as such we can be vulnerable to unscrupulous people. Because we want friends, but don't necessarily understand the boundaries or ins and outs of friendship, we can find ourselves in exploitative situations without even knowing it. Since, as already mentioned, some people on the spectrum try to buy their friendships through gifts and assistance, people can take advantage of this tendency. I have known people with autism who regularly meet up with 'friends' at bars and restaurants and routinely pay for everything because they think that these are the terms of the relationship, without realizing the 'friend' is taking advantage of them. I know several people with autism who have loaned large sums of money to 'friends' that they never saw again. I guess the solution to this is that when you meet up with people, always pay your own way and never lend money. True friends will understand, and if they do not then they are not your friends.

As people who do not always understand social rules, people with autism can also be easily manipulated for amusement or more nefarious purposes. More socially skilled people can set us up by telling us to say something; only when we do, it does not have the meaning we think it has and we either make a fool of ourselves or offend someone. I've met people who think it would be 'funny' to get an Aspie drunk or trick them into taking drugs to see the outcome. We can also be used by the opposite sex in complex relationship games. I knew one woman who tried to entice me into a secret relationship, played with my emotions and broke my heart, just to make her boyfriend jealous. Another time a female friend told me to make a move on a girl because 'she really likes you', which I did, only to discover that this girl had a boyfriend and the 'friend' was using me to try to break them up. We can also be drawn into antisocial or even criminal behaviour by people we think are friends, who are actually only using us as a convenient scapegoat. The problem is that, lacking the skills to deal with conflict, we struggle to extricate ourselves when 'friends' apply pressure or knowingly mislead us. People with autism, then, need to take steps to protect ourselves from such situations.

We must also be very careful not to be exploited when it comes to sex and sexual activities. Many people on the autism spectrum, both men and women, can be rather naïve about this topic, and this can make them a target for predators. Unable to find meaningful relationships in their everyday lives, yet desperate for them, people with autism can seek them out through dating websites, magazine ads, pornographic websites and premium-rate telephone lines, which exposes them to all kinds of financial and psychological manipulation. Often insecure and trusting of the other person's greater experience, we can accept at face value that certain things are 'normal' or acceptable when they are not, and we can be coerced into doing things that we are not comfortable with or do not approve of because we would rather do them than lose the relationship. People with autism are therefore particularly vulnerable in this area because sexual abusers can prey on our emotional needs. I would therefore highly recommend anybody with AS or ASD who is concerned or unsure of a situation to speak to trusted figures in your life, no matter how difficult that might seem, to make sure things are above board and acceptable. Likewise, pornographic websites and phone lines are not ideal places to meet life partners, and if you are meeting people from dating websites, be sure to take things slowly and meet in public places, at least until you know that you can trust them.

Sex

This brings us nicely onto the topic of sex. As mentioned in the previous section, people with autism can be remarkably naïve and uninformed about sexual matters, often unaware of our own bodies, needs and sexual desires. Sometimes this stems from a lack of interest and sometimes from a lack of opportunity. If you grew up without friends at school who discussed matters of a sexual nature in the playground, or an older sibling who had access to magazines that discussed them, then your knowledge of sex might have been limited to the bare-bones information that you were taught in school. Alternatively, many without sexual experience, and this is true of neurotypicals as well as Aspies, have warped, unrealistic and idealized interpretations of sex from the way it is portrayed in movies, on TV and, increasingly, on pornographic websites on the Internet. Whatever your knowledge base, it is normal and it is healthy for people with autism to want to have sex, and be interested in sex, but the reality is utterly different from the image.

There has been surprisingly little research done into autism and sex. In my (limited) experience, people on the autism spectrum can be unimaginative when it comes to sex. As with most social acts, sex requires effective communication and an ability to understand the needs of another person, and struggling in these areas, people with autism can therefore interpret sex in a goal-oriented, functional manner, as a mechanism for pleasure rather than a complex emotional bonding experience between two people. Focusing on the genitals and the act of penetrative sex until climax, since this is the basic definition of sexual intercourse, the autistic partner can lack an appreciation of the surrounding features of sex, such as emotional closeness, intimacy, foreplay, experimentation, the art of romance, cuddling, kissing, paying attention to other parts of the body and an intuitive meeting of the partner's desires. This is not to say that we are necessarily bad or selfish lovers, and we can certainly learn about sex intellectually, in the same way we learn about every other aspect of social life, and adjust our behaviour to get 'better' at love-making, but it is not something that comes naturally to us. As an analogy, I explain sex as being like you have been invited to someone's house for a drink. The autistic partner will often walk straight into the kitchen, open the fridge, grab the drink, drink it and leave. What we need to learn is that first we have to ring the doorbell and wait for an answer, then when we enter the house we have to take off our coat, and we have to sit down and make small talk and chit-chat until we are invited into the kitchen and offered a drink. And afterwards, we have to make more small talk and more chit-chat before we put our coat back on and go. Sex is therefore a drawn-out social process.

People on the spectrum often do not have overpowering physical desires that need spontaneous fulfilment in the way that is often depicted in neurotypical relationships. Sometimes, people with autism will have no thoughts or desires for sex, and this is by no means wrong. At other times, sex can be treated as a run-of-the-mill part of a relationship, no different to washing the dishes or going through the bills, something that one ought to do because it is expected rather than something you actively feel a need for. Indeed, people with autism can treat it as something that is scheduled in – we haven't had sex for a few days so in order to meet the national average for relationships, we'd better have sex tomorrow night. If our partner wants sex, we can go along with it, but if it was not a regular occurrence then it probably wouldn't bother us. This is not to say that we don't want sex, but it is not always high on our list of priorities in a relationship. It is important, therefore, for the neurotypical partner to be explicit about their needs. While it can be embarrassing to talk about such intimate issues, if we are mature enough to have sex then we are mature enough to talk about it.

Confusion around our sexual identity, desires and needs is also common among people with autism. As noted before, often unable to understand our emotions or whether we are drawn to a person because of a desire for friendship or sexual attraction, we can be unsure whether we are straight, gay, bisexual or asexual. Many on the spectrum will have had crushes on both males and females, whether or not they have acted upon them. For example, before I was married, when I was drawn to a woman and wanted to hang out with her, I assumed it was because I was sexually attracted to her and acted accordingly. When I was drawn to a man and wanted to hang out with him, it confused me as to what I wanted out of the association and I wondered if I was sexually attracted to him, although in retrospect, it was simply a desire for friendship that I misinterpreted as a desire for a relationship. If I think of many of my past romantic relationships with women, they were actually more like friendships in which we had sex. Some of my 'romantic' relationships never evolved beyond the peck-kissing stage, and in hindsight should be regarded as friendships. Unfortunately, therefore, sexual confusion appears to be a relatively common part of having autism.

At the same time, sex is just one part of life and not everyone feels comfortable with it. It can be very difficult for somebody with AS or ASD to relax enough to be close to another person, particularly when naked, which can leave them feeling vulnerable and exposed. Some people with autism can be extremely sensitive to touch and stimulation, struggling to contain their feelings when they are being cuddled or stroked, and to these people, sex is an intolerable thought. Conversely, other people can be dulled to their senses so that it takes a great deal of stimulation for them to feel anything – for these people, sex can seem a pointless endeavour. The sights, sounds, smells, tastes and touches of sex can be overwhelming, bewildering or unpleasant, and we will all enjoy different things or nothing at all. Like every aspect of a relationship, there is no rule that says it has to be a certain way, and since sex is an act between two people, it needs to be negotiated and modelled into something that suits both parties.

People with autism can, however, be at the opposite end of the sexual spectrum, holding unhealthy attitudes towards sex and behaving in inappropriate ways. Having learned about sex from pornography, for example, they can believe that aggressive, violent, over-the-top sex with an alarming disrespect for their sexual partner is normal. They can also be careless or oblivious towards social norms, acting promiscuously or being indifferent towards nudity, walking past open windows while undressed, either without being aware or without caring that they can be seen naked; or sending explicit photographs to potential sexual partners; or displaying sexually aggressive courtship behaviour. Since people with autism are prone to obsession, they can become obsessed with sex and sexuality, learning everything they can about it, and talking about it at every opportunity in a manner that makes others uncomfortable. Similarly, they can become obsessed with the act itself, becoming addicted to pornography, sex lines and online live video streaming, running up large bills and exposing themselves to potentially dangerous practices. Some with autism will engage in sexual acts or masturbate in public places, and while there are plenty of neurotypical people who do this too, for the person with AS or ASD it is often down to a lack of awareness of societal norms and poor impulse control.

The thing that some people with autism struggle to remember is that while sex is normal, there is a time and a place for it, and there are laws restricting inappropriate behaviour. While in movies 'no' can be taken as 'yes', stalking a person often leads to them falling in love with you, and ripping off your potential partner's clothes without a word being spoken is perfectly acceptable, in reality these actions can and most likely will get you arrested. Whenever you consider engaging in sexual activity with other people, consent must always be obtained first, and the limits of the activity understood. Never assume that you understand another person's intentions, because we are not great at making these independent interpretations, and a nod, eye contact, or whatever other non-verbal signals you think might represent consent could have been misinterpreted. When in doubt, always ask for consent.

The partner with AS or ASD

There is no barrier separating one type of person from another and people with autism can have friendships with both neurotypical people and those on the spectrum. When it comes to sexual relationships, however, some people frown upon a neurotypical being with an Aspie as the former is obviously more socially experienced and comfortable with these types of association than the latter. I have even met people who have described this as a form of abuse, as though a neurotypical attracted to an Aspie is somehow exploitative and sinister. There are psychologists that claim NTs who love Aspies are drawn to them as they need someone to look after and feel superior to in order to bolster their own self-esteem, while Aspies loving NTs are seeking parent figures to look after them and guide them through the social world, as though an autistic–neurotypical relationship is a psychological condition. The fact is, however, that we are people, the same as any other, and we will be attracted to neurotypicals and Aspies alike, just as we can be attractive to neurotypicals. Sure, there might be a degree of truth in the idea that we fulfil one another's needs, but sexual and romantic attraction is less rational than that and far from explainable. Furthermore, in every sexual relationship there is one partner who is more experienced and capable than the other, but it does not follow that this individual is something other than caring and loving and genuine. While it is true that those of us with autism must be careful, I don't believe there is anything wrong on either side if we have relationships with neurotypicals, and many successful marriages and partnerships are of this kind.

As previously discussed, the partner with autism can be ignorant of some of the things that are expected in neurotypical relationships. Demonstrative love can be missing since we think the fact that we love you does not need any further embellishment. Given our social anxieties, many people on the spectrum prefer to socialize just with their partner, which can be frustrating and isolating for the neurotypical partner. Many autistic–neurotypical couples therefore socialize separately, with the NT partner going out with their friends or family and leaving the Aspie partner at home. We often won't mind this, but to the NT partner it can feel as though you don't appreciate their social needs. When they return from work we can launch into the middle of a deep conversation because we haven't seen them all day and want to talk to them, but in our enthusiasm we don't realize that we ought to give them a moment to catch their breath, make them a drink, and let them make small talk to unwind first. With black-and-white thinking we can get hung up on fairness, failing to make allowances for unforeseen events – if it is their turn to cook dinner, for example, the fact that they are tired does not seem a valid excuse because we were tired yesterday when it was our turn to cook but we still did it. Nor do we accept last-minute changes of plan. We can be overly sensitive and we misinterpret the things that they say. We are hung up on our interests and aren't interested in theirs. And they often mediate for us with the social world, so it is no surprise that it can be difficult and draining being the partner of somebody with autism.

As you might have noticed, the previous paragraph depicts autistic–neurotypical relationships entirely from the side of how hard it is for the neurotypical partner. This reflects much of what you will find in books and online about romantic relationships with Aspies. It is assumed that, as the partner with autism, you are the weaker, needier one who takes, takes, takes, while the NT partner does all the giving. The NT partner is praised for being able to put up with you, and you should feel lucky that somebody cares. Everything that you do is somehow 'wrong' because you are the one that is different, not the neurotypical partner. And since you are the one whose behaviour is odd, you are the one that needs to make extra efforts to accommodate the neurotypical partner and become more 'normal'. There are support groups for partners of Aspies, and advice to us on how to act. You should behave in this way or that way, should care more, should be more sensitive – essentially, you should be something that you are not. One wonders why, if some of these people are so desperate for a neurotypical partner, they were ever attracted to a person with autism in the first place!

While you should certainly listen to your partner, as they might be more capable in the social world than you are and because listening to one another is what relationships are about, I do not think that people on the autism spectrum should delegate all their authority and ideas on how to act to another person. In relationships you are both equal partners, or at least, you are meant to be. One will be better than the other at some things and vice versa, but as individuals you need to find a way of making the relationship work for both of you. It does not matter if it is an autistic–neurotypical or neurotypical–neurotypical relationship, all people have to compromise and adapt to their partner's needs to form a mutually beneficial, positive, rewarding, committed and loving alliance. Both sides need to accommodate the other. This might mean that, if you have AS or ASD, you could perhaps go out once a week with your partner so that their need to socialize as a couple is met, while they agree to make plans in advance so that you have time to prepare. These compromises are true of all relationships, and if either of you is unwilling to move your position towards the other then it is unlikely that the relationship will work.

Despite all the negative press, I do not think that having autism is in any way a barrier to a successful relationship. In my experience of having relationships with neurotypical people before being diagnosed, we communicated about what we wanted and adapted the relationship to suit both partners, and I think that is natural and normal. I was rather neurotic and anxious about doing the right things and often 'flew off the handle' over misinterpretations, but they were happy, mutually supportive relationships that were based on shared interests. They were not very passionate and fizzled out when we realized we had become best friends instead of lovers, but like most people with autism I was loyal and committed and wanted to be a good partner, so was prepared to do the things that my partner wanted, provided she told me what those things were (such as buying flowers). Indeed, the neurotypical in a relationship with a person with autism may need to be more explicit about their needs than they would in an NT-NT relationship, may have to be blunter, more direct, and tell you if something needs doing. If they want somebody who intuitively understands and meets their needs and approaches the relationship in an emotional manner, then having a partner on the spectrum is probably not ideal. However, if they can bring themselves to communicate what they want, this is a small concession for having a partner who is loyal, reliable and committed.

On the other hand, there are, undoubtedly, some people with autism who make terrible partners, being selfish, needy and inconsiderate. It is a myth that in a 'good' relationship you never fall out or have to compromise, and if you are not prepared to make any changes to enable you to have a successful romantic relationship then perhaps you should not have a relationship at all. I don't mean to be harsh, and I'm not advocating you betray your ideals and sense of identity, but a relationship is about two people and if you want it to work, you have to put in the work. Many people with autism believe that they are correct 100 per cent of the time, and cannot conceive that other people can have a legitimate alternative idea. For example, a neurotypical partner might tell their autistic partner that they are not being made to feel very loved; the autistic partner thinks that they are doing enough to make the neurotypical partner feel loved, and therefore dismisses their partner's concerns as 'wrong'. Similarly, since people with autism are often committed to fairness, we can misunderstand that what is fair to one person may not be fair to another. If we have no desire for friends and only need our partner for social stimulation, for example, we can think it unfair that our partner needs friends. We can similarly resent our partner's going out when we never do because it is unfair, even though we don't *want* to go out ourselves. An autistic partner can therefore be unreasonable and difficult.

People on the spectrum can also be hypersensitive to criticism, and because of the way we think often overreact to simple, innocuous statements. This comes from our difficulties understanding how other people are thinking and feeling. For example, if we take our partner cycling and after several miles they say, 'Wow, this is hard work,' we can interpret this to mean that they aren't enjoying themselves. From there, we decide that our partner must therefore hate cycling, and if that is the case then they must think our ideas for activities are rubbish. If they think the activities we like are rubbish then they must hate being with us. If they hate being with us it means they don't really love us.

And so the autistic partner responds to the statement, 'Wow, this is hard work,' by saying, 'Fine, if you don't want to be with me any more, we should just separate.' In this manner we have ignored all the signs that they are enjoying themselves and, using faulty logic, have twisted their innocent statement into a vast, paranoid conspiracy. The partner with autism can often leap to these unfounded conclusions and therefore we need to be very careful not to allow our way of thinking to ruin pleasant occasions. I have assured my autistic wife that if I no longer love her, I will tell her, so she doesn't need to keep asking me why I don't love her any more!

In part, however, some of the supposed problems with dating an Aspie can be the result of the neurotypical partner's assumptions about our abilities, or their unwillingness to communicate when things are wrong. In my first relationship I fell into a system whereby she started to do everything for me and I let her – I thought that was the role she wanted. Later, during an argument, she told me how frustrated she was that I never did anything for her; it was an eye-opener for me because I hadn't realized that there was anything wrong. Having been told of this problem, I adapted my behaviour to make sure I met her needs, and the relationship was better afterwards. Therefore, provided both sides have a genuine commitment to one another, with love and respect and a willingness to communicate, there are few obstacles that cannot be overcome.

AS and AS

I have heard it said many times, by professionals who work in the field, family members and people with autism, that 'AS and AS doesn't work'. The same applies for 'ASD and ASD'. There is a pervasive idea that two people with autism cannot possibly have a healthy, mutually supportive or successful romantic relationship because, each with their own problems to deal with, they will exacerbate one another's condition. There is also, I think, a deal of fear among professionals and family members because our relationships do not resemble 'normal' relationships and they worry about having to deal with fallout if things go wrong. It is true that our relationships with one another can be volatile, unstable and emotionally damaging, but so can anybody's. If it were impossible for people with autism to have positive relationships with others with the condition, then I would not be married to my wife, and we are certainly not unique.

There are many positives to having two partners with autism in a relationship, and the structure the relationship takes is open to negotiation. I have come across a couple, for example, who are quite open about their pragmatic meeting of one another's needs – she wanted somebody she could do things with, and he wanted somebody he could have sex with. Their relationship does not appear to be particularly emotional, but they are devoted to one another and seem perfectly happy. They have created a committed relationship that is totally unromantic, but it works for them, and even if people cannot understand it from the outside, it is nobody's place to judge.

Another key advantage of this kind of relationship is that, if we are educated about our condition and open to learning, we can understand our partner and they can understand us, enabling us to make allowances for one another. Our autism affects my wife and me differently, and we are by no means similar, but when she is freaking out over something trivial, or refusing to go to bed until she has found the puzzle piece she is missing, I can understand why. This also feeds back into my own understanding of my condition by showing me the effects of my behaviour on others. We therefore learn about one another and ourselves through our autism, and grow as a couple and as individuals in response. Indeed, several of the people who were against us getting together in the first place have later commented how good we have been for each other. We might be naïve, and sometimes it is like the blind leading the blind with us, but we muddle through and have achieved things together neither of us would have been capable of individually.

I am aware, however, that we are not the norm, and our relationship is not always easy. We frequently fail to understand one another's intentions, misinterpret what we say and thus take offence at imaginary slights, and lack the skills to bring the conflict to a speedy resolution when we fall out with one another. Sometimes our behaviours will bounce off each other and cause us to 'act out', and when we both think we are right we don't have the good sense to back down. While we have enough self-restraint, genuine affection and commitment to one another to ultimately resolve these problems, this is not always the case with every autistic couple. I know several people who have been in autistic relationships who were unable to support one another and whose autistic tendencies wound each other up so much that they rowed all the time. Since people on the spectrum can have all-or-nothing tendencies, we often fall in love quickly, throw ourselves wholeheartedly into relationships, and refuse to let go when they don't work; and when both partners do the same, the results can be explosive. There are many in the autistic community who have been hurt as a result and now counsel against all autistic relationships. But, as I maintain, it is down to the individuals and their willingness to make exceptions for one another. If you are genuinely committed to each other, it is certainly worth giving it a go.

Domestic abuse

In recent years in neurotypical society, the definition of domestic abuse has expanded from physical violence to the propensity of one partner to dominate and control the other through a variety of psychological, verbal and emotional behaviours. These include humiliating or ignoring your partner, withholding affection until you get your own way, ignoring your partner's interests or accomplishments, acting jealously or obsessively, preventing your partner seeing family or friends, limiting their access to money or transport, treating them as an object, and blaming them for any violent outbursts until they believe that they have brought it upon themselves and deserve it. This list is, unfortunately, markedly similar to some of the behavioural traits of a partner with autism. However, the question to ask is whether something is 'abusive' because of the intention behind it or the effect it has on others.

There are two extreme positions regarding domestic abuse in relationships with people with autism. One of them is that people on the autism spectrum are by our nature abusive in our behaviours and anybody in a relationship with an Aspie is abused. The other is that as people with autism cannot help our behaviours, it is wrong to label anything we do as 'abuse', even if we lash out in an 'autistic meltdown' and strike our partner. I think both positions are wrong. When we are not deliberately trying to control our partner and are oblivious to their distress, it is difficult to argue that our behaviour is abuse because it is not consciously done and it is not our intention to cause hurt; equally, it is dangerous to suggest that somebody with autism can treat their partner in any manner whatsoever without its being construed as offensive, especially when it comes to violence. As with most things, the reality is somewhere in-between.

To a certain extent, some of these supposed 'abusive' behaviours of autistic partners can be the result of misinterpretations. If you refuse to socialize with your neurotypical partner because of social phobia, this can be interpreted as 'you won't let me see my friends'. The truth, however, is that you simply refuse to socialize and your neurotypical partner doesn't want to socialize without you and so *chooses* not to. In a similar way, if you don't encourage or pay attention to your partner's interests, they can interpret this as 'you belittle my interests', when in reality you are genuinely not interested. Neither situation is ideal for the neurotypical partner, but rather than abuse, this is simply the result of different ideas about what is important in a relationship. This is why communication is so important, because it may well be that, as the autistic partner, you are unaware of the effect of these behaviours. Similarly, obsession with your partner or treating them as an object instead of a complex emotional being are common with autism, and unless you're made aware that these behaviours are having a negative impact, you may well continue in a state of ignorance. All autistic partners therefore need to encourage their significant others to communicate their needs in an open and honest manner.

Notwithstanding the above, partners on the autism spectrum can indeed fit a definition of 'abusive'. As a result of problems understanding how others think and feel, people with autism are often unable to appreciate the cares, concerns and needs of another. We can therefore be blunt, cold, unappreciative, belittling, unsupportive and aggressive. Thinking we are right all the time, we can be unwilling or unable to accept when we are behaving unacceptably, and think our partner unreasonable if they protest at our treatment of them. This can even exacerbate the situation as, unable to see things from our partner's point of view, we stubbornly adhere to a course of action that we are determined is 'right', making it even worse in the long term. Indeed, with a warped idea of fairness, some with autism can justify almost any abuse. For example, if you work all week, you can think that the weekend is 'my time' and therefore anything your partner wants from you at the weekend is unfair. No matter how nastily you behave, you can justify it as your partner is the one being 'unfair' and you are simply fighting for your rights. Blaming your partner for your own aggressive and controlling behaviour is very much the definition of an abuser, and cannot be ignored just because you have autism.

People on the spectrum are also more likely to become frustrated as a result of not being able to deal with stress and the fact that we do not understand our emotions. Furthermore, once we have reached a state of anger, we find it very difficult to control ourselves. An angry, aggressive, out-of-control and violent Aspie is not nice to be around. Having a partner can cause increased stress, which can make us more likely to become agitated. It is up to people with autism to learn to control themselves at such times and remove themselves from the stressful situation. If you do lose control, your neurotypical partner, as the 'cause' of the stress, can become the focus or target of your rage. In no way is this acceptable. If a person with AS or ASD is unable to control their temper, they should not be in a relationship; but unfortunately, many will not have the self-awareness to realize how destructive and damaging their behaviours can be.

SUMMARY

- Most people with high-functioning autism want friendships and relationships.

- We often try to think our way through friendships and relationships and struggle to accurately define their boundaries.

- We are vulnerable to exploitation, but can be obsessive, unsupportive or abusive partners ourselves.

- We can have issues around sex and sexuality.

- Communication is key to all healthy, functioning social relationships.

CHAPTER 8

The Parent with Autism

If you ask any parent what it is like to have a child, they will say that, while it is rewarding and exciting, it is also extremely difficult. This is true for neurotypicals and Aspies alike, and the difficulties change with the age of the child – a newborn baby presents a whole different set of problems from a seven-year-old, just as the seven-year-old is entirely different from a teenager. For people on the autism spectrum, however, there are added difficulties to being a parent that stem from the condition. Many people with autism have children – indeed, I have a lovely neurotypical daughter – and there is nothing to say that if you have autism you won't make a great parent, but it is important to be aware of the issues and how they affect both parent and child in order to mitigate any negative consequences.

Since the realm of parenting is so broad, it would take an entire book to describe how AS and ASD affect every aspect of parenting at each stage of your child's life. Furthermore, there is no 'ideal' model of parenting, so each parent works out their own way of dealing with their children – what works for one won't work for another. This chapter therefore covers some of the key problems you might face as a parent with autism, difficulties that might arise with your partner, and how to meet your child's salient needs, but is in no way exhaustive or complete. If you are a parent or are planning to be one, I would strongly recommend consulting books on parenting and child development to understand what your child needs from you.

Deciding to have children

I've heard it said that an autistic parent raising a neurotypical child is the 'definition of abuse', which shows that while for most humans having a child is something completely natural, if you want a child when you have autism then you need to be prepared for unsupportive reactions, doubts and concerns. If you are being supported by a social worker, you may find you are asked to jump through a number of hoops to prove that you understand what you're getting yourself into and that you have the requisite skills to become a parent. Do not be surprised if the unborn child is assigned their own social worker to safeguard their interests while they assess you. This can continue after the child is born, with people checking to make sure your child is reaching the social and developmental milestones, which is not necessarily a bad thing but can make you feel a little patronized. Clearly, there is a great deal of negativity surrounding autism and parenting, and some people try to discourage those of us on the spectrum from procreating altogether.

Many of these concerns are understandable, however. Since most of us with autism like stability and routine, don't like change, struggle to adapt to new challenges, and are sensitive to certain noises and smells, it is legitimate to consider how we will cope with the disruption that babies cause to our lives. Babies are by their nature unpredictable, and the world becomes unpredictable when you have them. Visitors arrive with little or no notice, the dinner you usually eat at six grows cold as you deal with your child, and long-held plans have to be dropped without warning. Furthermore, if you struggle to look after yourself, how will you look after a baby? Parenthood is one of the hardest things I have ever had to do, and it is not for everyone. This is not to be unduly negative: it is to ensure that anybody with autism considering having a baby understands the sacrifices they will have to make and the difficulties they will face, and makes a reasoned, realistic decision.

For some people with autism, focused on their own hobbies and interests and unable or unwilling to compromise on their time and space, having a child is not to be recommended. On the other hand, with a willingness to undergo hardships and an understanding that it will not be easy, others are able to learn to cope with their routines being torn asunder and their obsessions being neglected, at least until other routines can be put in place and stability of a kind can once more reign. Obviously, neurotypicals face the same upheavals in their lives when a baby arrives as we do, and just as some of them cope admirably while others flounder and cannot manage, so some with autism are fully capable of adapting to the demands of a child while others cannot. This is the crux of the issue: nobody knows beforehand how they will react, but provided you are entering parenthood with an open mind, an awareness that things will change drastically, and a desire to be a good parent, then I don't think there's anything to say a person with autism cannot learn to manage.

A genetic basis for autism

Many parents with autism worry that they'll pass it on to their children. Having a baby is never without risk, whether you are on the autism spectrum or not. Anecdotally, many of us with AS or ASD have noticed autistic traits in our parents and believe that they or aunts and uncles might be on the spectrum, suggesting a genetic basis for autism that could be passed on. Currently, however, there is no evidence to suggest that people with autism are any more likely to have autistic children than other sections of society. Whether you take that risk is entirely up to you, but to a certain extent it depends on how you feel about your autism. If you see it as a negative trait that you would not wish on anybody then you might not be prepared to risk having a child with autism; if, despite making life more complicated, you accept your autism as being part of you, you might be more prepared for the possibility. Since I value my life and believe that I have as much right to it as anybody else, in spite of my autism, I was prepared to risk passing autism onto the next generation when I had my child. And if my child did grow up on the autism spectrum, then who better to understand how they felt, and guide them through the ups and downs of living with the condition, than somebody who has had to face it themselves?

Meeting your child's needs

There is often concern over whether a parent with autism will be able to meet the emotional and social needs of their children. There are websites that warn that children of autistic parents feel a lack of emotional closeness growing up because while you might love them, you do not demonstrate it in a way that is understandable to your child. The neurotypical partner has to go overboard with signs of affection in order to compensate for your lack of it, and this can create tension within families. There are also doubts about whether you will be capable of giving appropriate support during difficult times or at developmental milestones. Some even claim it is inevitable that autistic parents will cause long-term psychological damage to their offspring, a conclusion that, as a parent with autism, I find particularly unjust.

I do believe, however, that parents on the spectrum need to pay close attention to our behaviour and the expectations of parenthood. It is no good 'winging it' and hoping things will turn out okay. All parents are limited by their own viewpoint and understanding, and through no fault of your own you may find that because of your autism you struggle to be aware of your child's needs. In order to develop into psychologically healthy adults, children need things like love and hugs, physical contact and smiles to reassure them that all is well. They need praise and support alongside correction. They need to be spoken to, listened to and understood, and they need the opportunity to mix with others, make friends and learn about socializing. These are all things that parents with autism do not often instinctively understand or cater for.

Because of your autism, as a parent of young children you might struggle to 'get' that though the bathwater isn't too hot for you, it might be too hot for them, or you might not understand how to dress them appropriately for the temperature. If you're planning to take the child somewhere but they get tired and stroppy, you might still go because you hate change and can't empathize with your child's discomfort, when really you should let them sleep. If you have a routine mealtime and the child refuses to eat, you can interpret this as the child being disobedient and try to force them to eat, when in actual fact they are feeling unwell, don't like the food or simply aren't hungry. While these behaviours are often neither deliberately neglectful nor necessarily harmful for the child, not being able to see or prioritize your child's needs is not a good thing in the long term.

As our children become more emotionally complex, we are often unable to pick up on the subtle hints and small clues that indicate their emotional state, and can therefore be oblivious to their feelings. It is often easier to work out what is wrong with pre-verbal children, where communication is limited to crying and their needs are mostly physiological, than with older children who are able to articulate their needs but might not express them explicitly. For example, you might interpret your ten-year-old's lack of conversation to mean that everything is fine, when your neurotypical partner might realize that this means there is something on their mind that is troubling them. We can struggle to understand where our child is coming from, how they are feeling, or what they want from us.

That said, it is entirely possible as parents with autism to consciously learn to interpret the behavioural signs of our children, and over time many become experts at 'reading' our offspring. Certainly, your skills improve with experience, you start to understand how and why your child acts the way they do, and you can adapt your behaviour to meet their needs. You also need to use your intellect to compensate for your inability to innately understand your child in the way a neurotypical parent might. I get advice from other parents, books and the Internet to make sure I'm considering and meeting my daughter's needs, and my life as a parent is therefore one of rules, lists, study and hard thinking. Aware of the tendency of autistic parents not to be demonstrative in their love, for example, I make sure I express my love in explicit ways, smiling and hugging and kissing and cooing, so my daughter doesn't feel unloved. If she brings home a picture from school that I think is rubbish, I will tell her it is good and put it on the fridge as I have learned that we need to bolster our children's self-esteem. Moving forwards, I will encourage her to communicate her needs in an open and honest fashion, without judgement on my part, to enable me to be an effective parent. No matter how unnatural these things might seem to you, or how uncomfortable you feel doing them, if you want to be a good parent and have a positive relationship with your child, you need to put in the effort to learn what children need at all stages of their development and try to meet these needs as they appear.

It is important to realize, however, that we can never meet every one of our child's needs. We will make mistakes, we will do things wrong, and we will miss things, but this is true of all parents, and provided we acknowledge these mistakes and learn from them, we are on the right path. There will be times when you feel out of your depth and when you have no idea what to do, but so long as you have put a support structure in place to provide assistance in these moments, such as a grandparent, friend or neighbour on the end of the phone that you can call, or books you can turn to for advice, then in spite of your autism you are acting no differently to any other conscientious parent.

Child socialization

As they grow up, neurotypical children automatically learn the rules of the social world by playing with other children. One of the difficulties of being a parent with autism is that, in order to facilitate this process, you have to take your child to a place where they can mix with other children. Whereas for many neurotypical parents, parent–toddler groups are a great way to meet other parents and have a chat and a coffee while the children play, they can be excruciating for those of us on the spectrum. Entering a room with 30 screaming, volatile, smelly, colourful, boisterous and fast-moving terrors is an assault on the senses that is almost overwhelming, and yet, unless we have friends with children the same age as ours, these groups are a necessary evil that we must endure in order to properly look after our children.

The same is true as the child grows older. If they take ballet classes or karate, for example, you will probably find yourself waiting around with other parents and having to make idle small talk. Your child will make friends at school and you will most likely have other children round your house for meals, sleepovers and birthday parties, things that you need to allow for your child's healthy social growth. If you want your child to have the same upbringing as any other neurotypical child, you'll take them to the fair, the park, swimming lessons, the beach, all situations that can trigger the worst of your anxieties. As a parent with autism, every day I fight to keep my fears hidden and project an image of calm and confidence so that my daughter does not pick up on my hang-ups and react negatively to these socially 'normal' situations. This is one of the unseen burdens of being a parent on the spectrum.

In addition to the discomfort of the social space, for a parent with autism the whole socialization process can be stressful and confusing. I understand at an abstract level that my daughter has social needs, but I don't really understand what these are, so when I watch her play with other children I find myself growing incredibly anxious trying to work out what she's doing and why she's doing it. I'm always terrified she's going to hurt another child, or another child will hurt her, and I want to step in if she takes something from someone else or they take it from her. However, these are all normal behaviours that enable children to learn about how to interact with others, how to share, and how to empathize. Since I don't understand what is happening, my instinct is to direct her social encounters from an intellectual standpoint, so that I remain in control of them and can steer them into something I am familiar with, when I really need to allow her to figure things out for herself.

If you know anyone who is willing to take your child to parent–toddler groups for you, I would certainly advise availing yourself of this service. Once the child starts school they learn about socializing by being among their peers in the classroom and the playground, and from this stage onwards you need to be able to offer advice about appropriate social behaviours and guide them away from negative or antisocial traits. They will, however, develop their own distinct personality and manner of interaction that will differ from yours, and it may well be that their level of social understanding (their 'social intelligence') rapidly exceeds yours. One thing you need to remember, though, is that since this is not your area of expertise, the onus is not entirely upon you to create a fully socialized child. If you have a neurotypical partner or a support network of neurotypical friends, parents, siblings and other family, your child will learn social skills from interacting with them, and if you require further assistance to meet the social aspects of your child's needs then you should not allow fear or pride to prevent you from seeking it.

Child safety

Since people with autism often fail to spot dangers in looking after ourselves, when we are tasked to look after the safety of another we can often overlook or simply fail to see important 'common-sense' hazards. This can be compounded by motor clumsiness which makes it hard to safely handle our babies. My wife, for example, takes our daughter to swimming lessons and spends so much time watching the other students to make sure she's doing it right, she often fails to realize the baby's face is underwater. Furthermore, with often restricted diets, whether through allergy or dislike of taste or texture, we can subject our children to a similarly restricted diet. We can also be easily distracted, particularly if something triggers a sensory overload, and so can fail to notice our child wandering off. Because of social anxieties in public places we can become overwhelmed and panic, reducing our ability to be effective parents.

While parents with autism can be rather lax on child safety, on the other hand we can take it to the opposite extreme and metaphorically wrap our children in cotton wool. We can deny our child any risk to the point where we become unreasonable, preventing them from mixing with other children in case they catch something, refusing to allow them to travel in other people's cars, or go on theme park rides, or go swimming, because we deem the risk too high. We can become obsessive over hygiene and cleanliness, hover around them every second to make sure they don't fall and hurt themselves, and cover every hard surface with foam. This is particularly problematic when they are learning to walk, since toddlers fall over a phenomenal amount at this time as part of the process of learning, and it can be very uncomfortable for an autistic parent. As with many things, the best solution is to strike a balance somewhere between the two extremes.

One thing that most parents on the spectrum have in common is that we find it difficult to shift our focus from one subject to another, and this impacts our ability to multitask in caring for our children. When I look after my daughter, for example, that is all that I do – look after her. I am not capable of concentrating on anything else, whether it is reading a book, watching TV, browsing in shops or doing the washing up. If I move my attention onto something else I can neglect her, or look after her in an absentminded fashion, which is neither safe nor healthy. Therefore, when I take her to fairgrounds or restaurants or museums, I pay little to no attention to what I am there to see and do, and channel all of my attention towards my child. While this means that I miss many of the pleasures that are available for me to experience, it also means I keep her safe and my unsafe autistic tendencies do not hinder my ability as a parent. This is a sacrifice that I have chosen to make, and something all parents with autism need to seriously consider if they similarly struggle to multitask.

All-out parenting

The flipside of this coin is that, given our all-or-nothing thinking, problems with understanding relationships and propensity for obsession, parents with autism can become fanatical about the process of parenting. While I advocate an intellectual approach to parenthood since we often lack empathy and an intuitive understanding of our children's needs, the danger is that we can spend all our time considering and catering to their needs, and everything we do, think or feel revolves around them. Indeed, to do anything else or have any time off can feel like we are betraying them, and we sacrifice every aspect of our lives to focus on them. While you might think this makes us excellent, attentive parents, it is not necessarily a helpful or healthy trait.

Parents with autism can struggle to understand that time away from the child, allowing other people to look after them, is good for both of you. We can become very possessive of our children and want to be with them all the time, even preventing others from spending time with them, which has the adverse effect of not enabling the child to learn social skills or how to play by themselves, and harms their confidence and self-esteem. It also means that we neglect the other essential tasks of life – cooking, cleaning, paying bills – and even neglect ourselves. From experience, I have often been so focused on my daughter's needs, especially when she's ill, that I've forgotten to eat, drink or sleep for days at a time until I have collapsed.

Mental exhaustion is a very real risk for parents with autism. Since we generally process information in a more labour-intensive and time-consuming manner than neurotypical people, being a parent with autism places massive demands on your mental energy. Parenting, by its nature, involves interacting, communicating and forming a relationship with another human being, the very things autism affects. While we can consciously process those things that other people do automatically, it is a difficult and exhausting endeavour to consciously figure out thoughts, emotions and experiences at the same time as changing the baby, sterilizing bottles, taking the kids to the dentist and dealing with their friends being around the house. You can quickly find yourself physically, emotionally and mentally drained.

It is therefore important not to forget that, as an autistic individual, you have needs that relate to your condition. Most of us on the spectrum have various coping strategies that enable us to deal with the stresses of life and function on a day-to-day basis, such as doing a jigsaw puzzle or playing a computer game to 'switch off', or simply lying on the sofa staring at the ceiling for an hour while we process everything that has happened. Having a child inevitably disrupts our ability to do these activities with anything like the frequency or regularity that we could before, and since we have so little free time we can opt to cut them out of our lives altogether in order to focus on the child. It is, however, vital to maintain at least some of these coping mechanisms, giving yourself time to unwind, or it can be very easy to burn out and cease to function entirely.

Given our single-mindedness, parents with autism can also find it difficult to cope with the twin roles of parent and partner, such that we can neglect the latter entirely in favour of the former. It is commonly said that when you have a child you don't cease being a partner, but given the problems we have switching from one thought process to another, or considering the needs of two different people at once, we have a tendency towards ignoring the needs of our partners, or ceasing to treat them as an important part of our lives. As a parent it can be extremely hard striking an appropriate balance between the needs of our children, our partners and ourselves, but this is something those of us with autism need to think about and plan for. It helps to be able to timetable guaranteed slots where you can indulge your needs as a couple or an individual, such as letting the child's grandparents look after them one day a week, and turn this into a routine so that you do not neglect the other important parts of your life.

'My way is right'

A related problem to all-out parenting is that those of us with AS or ASD can find it difficult to understand how other people think and feel, or why they might want to do things differently to us. Coupled with a tendency towards black-and-white thinking, this means we think our way of doing something is best, and therefore 'right', which makes all other methods inferior, and therefore 'wrong'. When it comes to parenting, which is a partnership, this can place an awful strain upon the relationship.

The parent with autism can find it very hard to step back and allow the other parent to look after the child in their own way. This can take the form of taking over the childcare entirely or stipulating rules for how things 'should' be done. When I became a father I found myself constantly peering over my wife's shoulder, criticizing her for how she did things, trying to guide her to do things in the way that I did them, which I considered the right way. Unfortunately, this had the detrimental effect of undermining her confidence and damaging her relationship with both me and the baby.

An important lesson for autistic parents to learn is that the other parent's way of doing things is not wrong, or inferior, but simply different. You cannot stage-manage your partner's relationship with the child, no matter how much you might want to. They have as much right as you to experiment with different techniques to see what works for them, and it will be different to how you do things because their relationship with the child is different from yours. Remembering this helps to ease the tensions that often develop between parents.

Nor is this a problem that exists only between parents. Throughout the child's life you will encounter people and institutions with other ideas about childcare than your own. Grandparents, aunts and uncles, day care, school and friends' parents might all do things differently to how you would do them. Short of fighting each and every one to have things done your way, you need to learn to accept early on that there will be things you dislike in various aspects of your child's life, but provided they are not causing harm to the child then you have to let things go. It is a difficult lesson, and it is extremely hard for a parent with autism to give authority to others, but exposing a child to different influences is ultimately good for them.

Furthermore, while all of us are destined to come into conflict with our children as part of the process of growing up, especially when they are teenagers, the stricter you are with acceptable ways of doing things, the more opportunities there are for problems to arise. The child will have their own mind and their own opinions that will differ from yours. For example, you might think sports are stupid and you'd prefer your child to be into reading, but they might love sport and want to be part of a team. As a parent who wants to meet your child's needs, you might find yourself taking them to practice and watching matches, regardless of how you feel about it. Again, while you might think your way of doing things is right, provided your child's behaviour is not causing harm, then as an autistic parent you need to learn when to step back and allow them to develop their own ideas about life.

Fairness

Since people on the autism spectrum can have very logical, systematic and pedantic ways of seeing the world, we often regard fairness as a black-and-white, unbending entity, and this can lead to problems when co-parenting a child. If our partner goes out for the day with their friends for six hours, leaving us to look after the kids, we consider that the next day we should get six hours to ourselves while they look after the kids. Similarly, if we put the baby to bed one night, our partner should do it the next, and if we change a dirty nappy then the following one is their turn.

This is not how fairness works in real life, however, and turn-taking in looking after a child is not conducive to a happy or efficient relationship, as logical as it might seem. Different people have different capabilities and different amounts that they can give, and parenting is a partnership where you work towards the same goal – a happy and healthy child – and not a game of pass-the-parcel that can make older children feel like a burden. To illustrate what I mean, my wife needs more sleep than me and struggles to recover from a disturbed night, whereas I cope much better. I have therefore always 'done' the nights with the baby. It is very easy to think it unfair that she gets more sleep than me, but really she is giving what she is capable of giving and I am giving what I am capable of giving. While people with autism can get very caught up in the fairness or unfairness of the division of labour in parenting, you need to remember that you are not in competition with your partner and that your effectiveness as parents is in your combined total efforts, not in you both giving equally.

Coping with sensory issues

Due to our sensory issues, people with autism can often struggle with the smells, textures and sounds of early parenthood. I know a father with Asperger's who is unable to change his baby as he is very sensitive to smell and the odour of faeces makes him vomit; I know another autistic parent who has to walk away whenever her baby cries because the high-pitched sound of her child screaming induces actual pain. My own difficulty is with squidgy textures – I find it physically repulsive to walk through mud or touch raw egg or meat, and I have a borderline OCD about being dirty and contaminated with germs. I therefore really struggled with the weaning stage, since it involved mushy, slimy food being smeared all over my baby's hands, arms and face, and consequently on me too. Since these reactions stem from our senses, they are difficult issues to overcome.

It is important for a child to feel comfortable in their own body, however, and I was told early on that if I screwed up my face while my daughter was eating, or constantly wiped her clean between mouthfuls, or made 'yuck' sounds as she dribbled half-eaten food down her chin, I would pass on my own problems with cleanliness to her, and that is the last thing I wanted to do. I have therefore had to force myself to smile and act calmly and supportively as she eats, even while I want to run away and wash my hands. Unfortunately, as a parent with autism you have to be prepared to do those things that go against your nature and find ways of adapting – earplugs to take the edge off the screaming, a peg on your nose to avoid the smell, and swallowing down your disgust when your baby throws up on you.

Behaviours to avoid

One of the criticisms levelled against autistic parents is that we can interpret our child's intentions in a negative fashion, inferring deliberate misbehaviour when something was an accident or innocently meant. If our child does something that upsets us, we can believe they did it *in order to* upset us, instead of because they're absentminded, distracted or simply children being children. We also often believe that every event has a specific, logical and deliberate cause, so we need to be very careful not to arbitrarily blame our children for things beyond their control. Otherwise, they can grow up feeling misunderstood and resentful of parents who always treated them as though they were 'bad'.

We are also said to be rigid and inflexible, disciplinarian and aloof. We can be unpredictable to our children, difficult to read or understand, intolerant, unwilling to listen, obsessed with our own interests and given to confusing outbursts of anger or other emotions. To a certain extent, these accusations are fair, and we need to take steps to avoid them. For me, it came down to a choice. I decided that I would not allow my autism to harm my parenting abilities, and so I do whatever I can to act as 'normal' as possible in front of my daughter.

It is inevitable that, as a person on the autism spectrum, you will experience times of high stress while parenting and will react in inappropriate ways. The key is trying to anticipate these reactions and having meltdowns, panic attacks or other outbursts out of sight of your children. Given the amount of sudden change and disruption you have to deal with, parents with autism can often react with frustration or annoyance to these frequent interruptions, but this is not appropriate in front of your child. You can try to build routines into your new life, and indeed babies and children especially benefit from regularity and routine, but you need to be flexible. When I encounter unexpected change I therefore grin and bear it, fight through the stress and anxiety, and do what needs to be done. Later, when I get the chance, I try to recover from the disruption.

The same is true with anxiety. Going into public places, driving through unfamiliar environments and experiencing new things are all situations that I find nerve-wracking and often provoke stress reactions, such as hand-flapping and verbal snapping. However, our children look to us for reassurance in unfamiliar situations, learning how they should read an environment from our behaviours, facial expressions and tone of voice. I therefore force myself to act as though everything is fine and that I know what I'm doing in order that my daughter feels safe and comfortable and does not pick up on my anxiety or social phobia. Being a parent with autism requires a great deal of suppressing your natural inclinations, but since we are experts at masking our condition, this is something we are often very capable of managing.

Perfectionism is another trait to avoid. As our children develop, parents on the autism spectrum can become preoccupied with the visible, outward signs of achievement in their children and fail to value who they are as people. This can lead to us holding them to an impossible standard, constantly criticizing their behaviour as we try to guide them towards our version of 'perfection', and damaging their self-esteem by never giving them positive feedback about their achievements. Our honesty means we often say things to our children that we should keep hidden, and it is a particularly important lesson to learn how to tell a white lie.

This perfectionism does not only extend to our children, however. We can be extremely hard on ourselves, trying to be the 'perfect' parent and beating ourselves up for falling short of this ideal. Similarly, we can be hard on our partners for not living up to this model. As an autistic parent you can approach life incredibly seriously, and the key to being a good parent and having a positive family life is to relax a little and have some fun. You still need the serious times, but you also need to create happy memories for you all to share. Learning to listen and to share your thoughts and feelings in a constructive, calm and positive fashion will dispel many of the more unpleasant possibilities of autistic parenting.

SUMMARY

- Many people are against people with autism becoming parents.

- You need to use your intellect and advice from others to compensate for your natural parenting deficits and meet your child's needs.

- Time away from your child, allowing others to look after them, is healthy for both of you.

- As a parent with autism you often have to mask your symptoms.

- You and your child need to learn to communicate with one another in a calm, open and honest fashion.

Final Thoughts

So that, in a nutshell, is what it is like to have high-functioning autism, whether it is called Asperger's Syndrome or Autism Spectrum Disorder Level 1. If you've made it this far, you should know what the condition is all about, be able to separate the facts from the myths, and have gained an appreciation of how the condition can affect various aspects of everyday life. Living with autism is not easy, but nor is it a debilitating illness. How your autism affects you is individual to you, and learning about yourself is what makes you a successful human being. What you are capable of achieving is not contained in the pages of a book but in your own heart and mind.

The journey to the diagnosis is only the start of the rest of your life. With a bit of work, an openness to thinking about your condition, and a willingness to confront your fears and prejudices, there is no reason why you cannot seize the opportunities that life sends your way. Eight years after my diagnosis, I am in the best place I have ever been, with a wife and child and prospects that I never dreamed possible. This is open to all of us provided we accept who we are, embrace our condition, and never lose faith in ourselves.

All the best on the rest of your journey.